Sea Stories
and
Navy Tales

by

John J. Cline

Corpus Editus Books • San Diego, California

Sea Stories & Navy Tales
John J. Cline

Corpus Editus • San Diego, California

ISBN: 0615218504
ISBN 13: 9780615218502 (Printed Version)

Cover designed by Photo-Artist Marc Auth
www.authphoto.com

LCDR John J. Cline, USN
Official Navy Photograph

DEDICATION

This book is not about combat and war. Nor is it about crime and punishment.

Rather, this is a collection of short stories about people; Navy people for the most part, but others too. Mainly, they were people with whom the writer came in contact while providing physical security, law enforcement, antiterrorism, emergency management, and some principal protective services in and for the United States Navy.

This is dedicated to the U.S. Navy's Master-at-Arms, Physical Security Technicians (Warrant Officers), Physical Security Officers, Marines, and Navy civilian security personnel, whose mission it is to protect military and civilian personnel and the material resources used to safeguard our nation and our national interests both in the United States and abroad. Their stories remain largely untold.

This book is also dedicated to my wife, Pat, and our children, Pamela, James, and Raymond because along with me, they somehow managed to live through the sometimes wacky life of a sailor and Physical Security Officer.

John J. Cline
http://Idahoauthor.com

TABLE OF CONTENTS

PROLOGUE

I'm told that the difference between a fairy-tale and a sea story is that where fairy-tales start with the words, "Once upon a time," sea stories always start with the words, "This is a no shitter."

The teller of sea stories is in effect saying that the yarn is absolutely true; although he or she is also serving notice that some literary license may have taken place. In fact, the whole tale may be an outright fabrication. It is always up to the listener (or in this case, the reader) to determine how much of the story may be fiction.

These short stories are as accurate as my memory allows. However, the tales are also taken from my perspective. Others who were involved in the events described herein may remember them differently. I have diligently tried not to embellish on actual events. So, as you enter the realm of the Navy Physical Security Officer, remember that these are sea stories, and as such, you should consider that each one starts with the time-honored words, "This is a no shitter." Also, this is a book of memoirs, therefore, it is written in the first person. The experiences of my naval career were some of the best days of my life.

GO NAVY!

NOTE: This book was <u>written for a general audience</u>, and as such, does **not** contain the colorful sailorly language normally associated with many sea stories and Navy tales.

CHAPTER ONE

Chapter 1.1 Introduction

Three U.S. Marines were trying to beat the hot noon-time sun by having an early lunch and a couple of cold beers under an umbrella made of palms on the patio of a local South American restaurant. They would report for work providing security at the American Embassy in the early evening hours—something they had done for the past couple of years without incident. They likely didn't hear the bomb detonate, but shrapnel tore their bodies like shredded paper. Their bloodstained jeans and guayberas were testimony to the savagery of the unprovoked attack.

Terrorism did not begin on 9/11. Rather, the modern age of terrorism more likely started after WWII in Algeria and Puerto Rico. Americans have been the target of terrorism since the early 1950s. However, as long as the killings, hostage-takings, hijackings, and bombings were directed at foreign service workers, military personnel, and the occasional businessman or foreign-traveling American tourist, little in the way of national antiterrorism preparedness or readiness took place. As an example, the international community could not even agree on the definition of terrorism. Hence the saying, "One man's terrorist is another man's freedom fighter". Neither could our own federal agencies agree on a common definition—each agency having had its own version of what was terrorism based on its mission.

Those of us who are of a certain age can vaguely remember news reports of terrorist-directed activities against Americans and citizens of other countries. However, those terrorist activities seldom made the news for more than a day of media-generated sensationalism, so the news reports were quickly forgotten unless you were a victim's friend or relative.

Although the tales in "Sea Stories" are about everyday Navy life, my ultimate objectives in providing law enforcement and physical security have always been about preparing naval facilities and personnel—military and civilian—for the coming tsunami-like wave of terrorism. Prior to 9/11, those objectives were largely ignored.

I had served in the Navy from 1956 to 1960 and then returned to civilian life working as a firefighter and a police officer. I married a year before returning to civilian life; the union of which provided us with three children. With the inception of the Navy Police rating,[1] I decided that there might be some unique opportunities back in the Navy. So in 1973, at age thirty four, I accepted a two-year recall and returned to active duty as a Navy Police petty officer. Twenty-four hours later, the name Navy Police was changed to Master-at-Arms (MA).

The Navy had changed radically since the fifties. Drugs and racial tension filled the barracks and ships. Petty officers, even chief petty officers, no longer maintained discipline in the ranks. They blamed the Chief of Naval Operations, Admiral Elmo Zumwalt Jr., for eliminating their authority. However, nothing could have been farther from the truth.

Many of the enlisted and officer leadership simply weren't exercising their authority.

Following the 1972 riots on the USS Kittyhawk and unrest on the USS Constellation, Congress suggested that the Navy form a military police force similar to that of the Army and the Air Force. Navy brass didn't want any part of a military police force, but it bowed to the

---

1 A rating in the Navy is an occupation requiring specific job skills.

wishes of Congress and created the appearance (or the illusion) of such a military police force.

The Navy assembled a small cadre of Navy Police/Master-at-Arms with no authority except that given by the individual unit commanding officer (CO). It took nine years for the Navy to create an Operations Manual. MAs were pretty much on their own, with little or no guidance from the Department of the Navy.

I reported to Naval Station San Diego and was assigned to the Transit Barracks while undergoing processing back into the Navy. Processing included a new seabag of uniforms, sewing my former Navy occupational rating badge on the sleeves of dungaree shirts and uniform coats, a complete physical, dental exams, and inoculations. After processing, I traveled to Lackland Air Force Base to attend the new MA School in San Antonio, Texas.

Chapter 1.2 "Sailors Have More Fun"

(August 1973)

Evidently, many of the Navy petty officers who were to report to the Master-at-Arms School had the same idea while they went about preparing for their trip to Lackland Air Force Base. Before leaving for San Antonio, they stopped by the local recruiting office to procure a sizable quantity of "Sailors Have More Fun" bumper stickers. Combined, there were literally hundreds of the Navy bumper stickers, and the bumper stickers suddenly appeared everywhere on and off Lackland AFB.

Nothing was sacrosanct. Navy bumper stickers appeared in bars and restaurants, businesses, and on the rear bumpers of vehicles throughout the city. Some women even wore them on their jackets or on the seat of their pants. A new fad was started in San Antonio.

The placement of Navy bumper stickers went on for several weeks, but got out of hand when classmates plastered the commanding general's official car from stem to stern. Starting at the grille and ending at the trunk, not one inch of the government car was spared, except for a small strip on the driver's side of the windshield, allegedly to allow the driver to see to drive. The base commander was absolutely furious.

The MA School's Officer in Charge, a warrant officer, was called to the office of the commanding general where the Navy officer received the general's full verbal wrath, including a number of threats about abruptly ending the warrant officer's military career. The warrant officer subsequently called an "All Hands" meeting where he shared that wrath with the students. Suddenly, mere possession of a Navy bumper sticker was reasonable cause to suspect that the owner had participated in vandalizing the general's car. Everyone quickly ditched their bumper stickers.

Following the successful completion of school, I changed my uniforms to reflect the new rating, and returned to my home in San Diego to prepare for my first fleet assignment as an MA.

CHAPTER TWO

Chapter 2.1 USS Chicago (CG-11)

On a gray, San Diego day in December 1973, I reported aboard the USS Chicago (CG-11). The ship was one of the last of the WWII cruisers reconfigured to function as a modern missile cruiser.

Official U.S. Navy photograph

The ship was 674 feet long, 71 feet at its widest, and carried a crew of 1,200 men. At that time, the USS Chicago was known as "The World's Most Powerful Warship".

The Master-at-Arms force consisted of a Chief Master-at-Arms (CMAA) and four petty officers, all of whom (except for the chief) were temporarily assigned to the MA force for six months at a time for the purpose of maintaining order and discipline among the crew. After six months, the petty officers would return to their primary jobs in their regularly assigned division. I was the first professionally rated MA to be assigned to the USS Chicago.

BMCM Ken Morgan was the Chief Master-at-Arms. The designation BMCM means that he was a Boatswain Mate Master Chief Petty Officer – Master Chief, the highest level that an enlisted man could achieve. He was unofficially called "Gold Badge" because the badge he wore was gold-colored, while badges worn by petty officers were silver-colored. Officially, he was called, "Master Chief".

In 1973, Master Chief Morgan was probably in his early 50's. He was a big man, and by any measure, he was fat. But under the fat was hard muscle.

He had come up through the ranks as a boatswain mate when being tough was a basic requirement for anyone working in a ship's deck department. And he had the reputation for having been exceptionally tough in his youth.

He had mellowed some by 1973, but underneath, there was still that youthful toughness. He was not a man you would ever want to cross. No one on the Chicago ever tried.

Other than Master Chief Morgan and the four petty officers who were temporarily assigned to the MA force, no one took particular notice of my arrival on the ship. I was just another petty officer. Since I was the only one on the MA force with formal law enforcement experience, I was designated Command Investigator, meaning that I would investigate misdemeanor crimes and those felonies that the Naval Investigative Service (NIS) could not or would not accept. I was also responsible for training the temporary MAAs.

Together, we patrolled the ship, normally working 16-hour days at sea and twelve hour days in port. Every fourth day we stood duty, meaning we worked all night too.

The Naval Investigative Service (NIS), which was later renamed the Naval Criminal Investigative Service (NCIS) of television fame, was nothing like the television version of the agency. NIS/NCIS had no criminal pathologist or forensic laboratory.

In those days, NIS agents were not particularly well regarded by officers of other law enforcement agencies. Some Special Agents of the FBI and especially officers from local law enforcement regarded NIS only as "the agency that investigated gays in the Navy". That was really an unfair portrayal because NIS commonly investigated very serious crimes, but that was their reputation in the 1970's, long before the television show "NCIS".

NIS agents knew that they were generally ill-regarded, and for many, it affected their self-esteem. So they looked at the new professional master-at-arms, several of whom had more extensive civilian law enforcement experience than did many of the NIS agents, as a threat to their professional status as the Navy's criminal investigative agency. Most of the more senior NIS agents did have some civilian law enforcement experience, but the more junior agents, especially those who had come directly from the officer ranks of the Navy, didn't.

What many NIS Agents did have was arrogance. When they became NCIS, they also became known to local law enforcement officers as the agency that "Never Could Investigate Stuff" (NCIS).

(December 1973 - Assault and Battery)

For me, work began at lunch, soon after my arrival. Ten black sailors had formed a line across the after mess decks, blocking access to the scullery.[2] To get to the scullery, sailors would have to pass through the line of men who had established the after mess decks as "their" territory. You couldn't pass without their permission. They were in fact threatening everyone of different ethnicity.

A white sailor pushed his way through the line. He was assaulted and stabbed with a fork that had been altered to be used as a two-pronged pick, with which to inflict maximum damage to the victim.

I loudly ordered the sailors to "knock it off", and told the victim to report to sickbay. I handcuffed the suspect and walked him backwards with a wrist lock through the mess decks to the Master-at-Arms office where he was charged with assault and battery. That got everybody's attention. Suddenly, the entire crew had taken notice of my arrival on the ship.

The mess decks master-at-arms (not the same as the ship's master-at-arms) were then directed to keep the after mess decks clear at all times, except for those who were going to the scullery with their trays. That stopped the threatening gestures on the after mess decks, but did little to relieve racial tension on the ship.

(December 1973)

Rampant use of drugs was also a major concern. After several weeks of training the temporary MAs in basic self-defense and investigative techniques, the MAs started apprehending drug users. It was a busy time. It was also a dangerous time, especially at sea after dark.

---

2 The scullery is where sailors take their trays to be washed when they have finished eating.

Historically, there are cases where a disgruntled sailor would hit another sailor on the head with a dogging wrench[3] or a pipe and push the body over the side. It only takes a matter of seconds, and if watches[4] were not alert or did not hear the splash of the body hitting the water, the victim simply vanished. He would not be missed until his next watch or until he failed to report for work. Although the few such occurrences were actually murders, there was seldom any proof that a murder had occurred.

Sometimes the Navy took the easy way out and reported the missing sailor as a suicide. Real suicides, of course, happened too. Either way, such cases were rare.

Because the danger to the ship's master-at-arms was potentially great, I ordered all MA's to patrol the ship in pairs, especially at night when they went outside the skin of the ship.[5] Gold Badge convinced the captain and the executive officer that they needed to increase the size of the Master-at-Arms force to eight temporary MAs.

Instead of the normal three or four offenders a week facing Captain's Mast—an administrative hearing held by the commanding officer—there was an average of thirty or more offenders, mostly charged with the possession or use of drugs. The increased number of sailors being placed on restriction or going to the ship's brig also got everyone's attention. The chiefs and officer corps were continually upset because they couldn't get any work out of a sailor who was in the brig.

---

3 A dogging wrench is a pipe used to secure a watertight door.

4 There a many types of watches in the Navy. In this case, the watch would have the same meaning as a sentry.

5 The reference skin of the ship to a sailor means the hull and the superstructure. If you are on deck in the open air, you would be outside the skin of the ship.

The commanding officer could place an offender in the brig for thirty days, or he could assign the offender to the brig for three days of bread and water. The brig was run by the Marine Detachment. Now Marines are not particularly well known for being genteel, so Gold Badge had to visit the brig daily to check on the welfare of offenders. However, unless an offender gave the Marines a hard time, they really didn't mess with the "brig rats" very often.

Word of the shipboard drug investigations got to the Special Agent in Charge of the NIS office at NAS North Island where the USS Chicago was homeported. He decided to run his own drug investigation, capitalizing on what the ship's MAs had accomplished.

By prior arrangement with the Master-at Arms, ten NIS agents boarded the USS Chicago one Monday morning to interrogate the sailors who had been busted for the possession or use of drugs. As a result of the NIS interrogations, another sixty-five sailors were charged with the possession and/or distribution of drugs or narcotics. The chiefs and officers corps really got upset. Even with a crew of twelve hundred, losing sixty-five people punches a big hole in the work schedule. Some of the crewmen were placed on restriction, others went to the brig ashore, and still others, the distributors, were bound over for Court Martial, some sailors never came back to the ship; they were kicked out of the Navy with a General Discharge.

Chapter 2.2 The Drunk Gunner's Mate

The Chicago was moored with its port[6] side to the pier at Naval Air Station (NAS) North Island. It was one of my first duty nights. At about 0100, while walking along the port deck, I noticed that the five inch thirty-eight[7] was being trained on the City of San Diego.

---

6 The port side of the ship is the left side.

7 Port (meaning the left side of the ship) five inch 38 caliber gun

Gun movement was not unusual when maintenance was being performed, but after normal working hours, weapons personnel were supposed to clear any gun movement with the Officer of the Deck. I went to the quarterdeck, just to check, not really believing that anything was amiss. The Officer of the Deck (OOD) had not given permission to train the gun.

The OOD and I went to the Fire Control Center,[8] which was unlocked and unmanned. The Fire Control system had been forwarded so that the guns could be triggered from the gun tub.

Five inch 38 on the *USS Chicago* (CG-11)

We ran to the gun tub where a drunken second class gunner's mate was training the five inch thirty-eight on the El Cortez Hotel. It was one of the more prominent buildings on the San Diego skyline. The gunner's mate explained that a bartender had refused to serve him because he was drunk, and hotel security personnel had escorted him off the grounds. He returned to the ship, removed the keys from the dungarees of the sleeping duty weapons petty officer, and said that

---

8 Fire Control – the central control point for firing weapons (guns and missiles) on the ship

was going to "blow the El Cortez Hotel off of the face of the map". He grinned.

The drunken gunner's mate was placed in the brig for the night and went to Captain's Mast the next morning. He left the ship shortly thereafter. No mention was ever made of the incident again. However, changes were made regarding where the keys to the weapons spaces were kept after normal working hours. Could he have actually fired a shot?

Chapter 2.3 WESTPAC Deployment

In May of 1974, the USS Chicago and her crew deployed to the western Pacific. It was the first of many extended separations from friends and family.

The ship arrived in Subic Bay in the Philippines in mid-June. Liberty was a sailor's dream – wine, women, and song; the consequences of which caused me to work pretty much both day and night.

One evening, the commanding officer asked me to drive him to the Officer's Club in the CO's official car. Even the captain was not allowed to use the official car for personal business, such as going to the O'Club. On the way, the captain casually mentioned, "I understand you used to protect the governor of California when you were a state police officer."

"Yes sir".

The captain said, "I've always wondered how you guys could do all that fancy driving that you see in the movies."

"For the most part, Captain, cars in the movies are equipped with switches that allow the driver to use front and back brakes independently. But in an emergency, we can usually perform a K- turn, even in a car without special switches."

"What's a K-turn," he asked?

I spun the steering wheel and jammed on the brakes. Front and back brake pads furiously grabbed at drums and rotors to the point of overheating. The front of the car veered into the oncoming lane and the rear of the car began to slide around to where the front of the car had been moments earlier. Stomping on the accelerator, the rear of the car continued its semicircle until the direction of travel had reversed itself. The captain grabbed at the dashboard and said only, "Oh".

He was just a bit wobbly as he walked through the entryway to the O'Club.

Chapter 2.4 Weapons Qualifications

The Marines used part of their time during the workday at Subic Bay to qualify their personnel on the rifle and pistol ranges. The Marine Detachment CO authorized me to tag along and to shoot the qualification regimen, but the CO chided his Marines when it was later disclosed that I had the top scores with the .45 caliber pistol. The Marines never looked at me in quite the same way again. And they never did outshoot me on the pistol range, although they bested me often with the M-16 rifle. Of course word travelled throughout the ship and did nothing to hurt my already notorious reputation with the crew.

The ship set sail for the Indian Ocean as a part of Task Force 75, which included USS Fanning (DE-1076), USS Mackenzie (DD- 836), and the oiler USS Passumpsic (AO-107). We made port calls in Somalia and Aden for the purpose of demonstrating that "the Indian Ocean was not a Russian Lake."[9] On the way, we went through the Straits of Malacca, arriving in Karachi, Pakistan early in July.

---

9 According to both the Admiral and the ship's Commanding Officer (Names intentionally not provided to protect their privacy.)

Chapter 2.5 Karachi, Pakistan

(July 1974 – Memorandum: Not for official use)

One night, three days before the Chicago was scheduled to arrive in Karachi, I was summoned to the admiral's cabin. The admiral had deployed on Chicago as the Task Force 75 Commander. A ship's master-at-arms would normally have no contact with the admiral, so I was surprised when I got the call. I knocked on the admiral's door and entered when authorized. The admiral introduced himself and asked me to take a seat next to the captain. A steward brought us coffee.

"John", the captain said, "We've been requested to have the ship's band play for a state dinner when we get to Karachi".

"Sir, a Navy band didn't deploy with the ship."

"I know," said the captain, "but there are some instruments on board." All you have to do is to put a band together within the next three days."

I was dumbfounded to say the least. What did this have to do with law enforcement, I wondered?

I said, "Captain, in order to do this, I will need to use the Multiple Purpose Room (MPR) for the next three days and nights. I will also need to hold auditions tonight, which means that we will have to tell the crew that we will be holding auditions. Then the band will need to practice day and night for the next three days, which means that those who are selected won't be working their normal jobs."

The captain reached over and grabbed the 1MC[10] microphone from the bulkhead.[11] Handing me the mic, he said, "So tell them".

---

10 1MC is the designation for the ship's public address system.

11 The bulkhead is Navy-speak for a wall.

"Now hear this, at the direction of the captain, we are putting together a band to play in Karachi. Personnel with musical experience are asked to lay to the MPR with their instruments for audition."

The crew probably thought that the announcement was a joke as they were slow to respond. Before the night ended, however, about twenty musicians, most of whom played either rock and roll or country western music, responded to the call. So, two bands were formed: One played rock and roll, and the other played country western music. Of the twenty musicians, three men had professional experience. Two of the men with professional experience were selected as band leaders. The third musician was charged with producing the show and developing the play lists that would be used in Karachi. Each band played fifteen-minute rotating sets.

When the ship arrived in Karachi, the two bands were bused, with their instruments, to the dinner. They reportedly put on a great show. However, due to the proliferation of drugs in Karachi, I was not allowed to attend. Rather, I had to work.

It was in Karachi that the captain demonstrated that he was truly an excellent ship handler. A Russian ship and a commercial cargo ship were already tied to the pier. The space between the two ships was assigned to the USS Chicago. There was no tug boat to push the Chicago into its assigned berth. The captain threw small chips of wood into the water to gauge the current, and parked the Chicago between the other two ships as if he was driving a car. It is questionable as to whether Navy Captains today could equal his performance; especially with a vessel the size of more than two football fields in length.

(July 1974)

My first assignment when we pulled into any foreign port was to determine how easy it would be for the crew to buy drugs and narcotics. Usually the crew was still working, so I had a head start of at least an hour or so.

I changed into civilian clothes, checked out with the XO, and left the ship only to return within a few minutes. Startled, the XO looked up from his paperwork and said, "I thought you were leaving."

"I did," I said, placing three blocks of hashish on his desk.

"Where did you get these?" he asked.

"I got them from a stevedore on the brow."[12]

In Karachi, drugs, especially hashish, were available just about everywhere. The captain decided that more rigorous anti-drug controls needed to be implemented. Those controls included searching personnel as they returned to the ship. That meant that chiefs, officers, and senior petty officers had to be assigned to search duties. So instead of three fourths of the crew being on liberty each day, only half the crew would get to leave the ship. Nobody liked the idea of "port and starboard liberty," but some liberty was better than no liberty. So with grumbling, the increased controls were put in place. Even so, drugs got aboard.

The Navy had recently implemented a program of urine drug screening. When a certain number was rolled on a pair of dice, everybody with a Social Security number ending in that number had to urinate in a bottle to be tested for drugs and narcotics.

Someone substituted the dice with a set that didn't have the number two. No one ever looked to see if the dice had all of the numbers. The substitution was not discovered for at least a couple of weeks, so those with a Social Security number that ended with the number two, got away without being tested for drugs.

---

12 The brow is the plank placed from shore to the deck of the ship so that people can walk on and off the ship.

Not only was the urine test shipboard wide, but sailors retuning from liberty were subject to a urine test if their number came up. Of course, when the results came back, sailors found positive for drugs went to Captain's Mast. Repeat offenders might be bound over for Court Martial. A couple of hundred pounds of hashish, marijuana, and amphetamines were confiscated. Over a hundred sailors ended up at Mast. There were more drugs in Pakistan than any of the other WESTPAC ports of call, and even with the added search procedures, a fairly large cache of hashish made it aboard.

Chapter 2.6 Punched Out by the Commanding Officer

(July 1974)

The captain of the USS Chicago took the use of drugs on his ship very seriously.

That wasn't necessarily true of other commanding officers; some of whom chose to ignore the situation, hoping that the problem would resolve itself. One sailor had been caught using marijuana twice before. Both times, he was sent to Captain's Mast. His third trip resulted in an unforeseen event.

Gold Badge, who would normally attend Captain's Mast, was elsewhere on the ship, so I attended the hearing in his stead. The white uniform of the accused was dirty and wrinkled, and his deportment toward the captain was disrespectful. When asked why the accused was still using marijuana on the ship, the sailor answered, "You wouldn't have a drug problem on the ship if the MAs didn't look for it."

The captain's right hand was tightly clenched. He had been pushing the top of the podium closer and closer to the accused. Finally the captain snapped. His fist moved from his side toward the face of the accused.

Now you never touch the captain, not even to save him from making a monumental mistake. So the obvious course of action was for me to step forward and take the punch, which I did. The captain shouted for everyone to leave the cabin. I herded everyone out and started to leave when the captain said, "Not you, John."

The captain asked if I was okay. I assured him that I was fine. "You know, you probably just saved my career."

I said, "Well, Captain, we need to keep you in your day job because that wasn't much of a punch."

The CO looked at me with hard eyes, probably wondering if there was some underlying meaning. Various versions of the story got around the ship.

For several days, the story about the commanding officer punching out the MA was the main topic of discussion on Chi- town, the crew's nickname for the USS Chicago.

Chapter 2.7 Operation Penguin

By mid-July, the ship was in the Arabian Sea and in the Gulf of Aden. It was unbearably hot. Sand that was picked up by winds blowing across deserts saturated the air around the ship; sometimes to levels as high as 30,000 feet. Sand infiltrated critical ship's equipment, which had to be cleaned several times a day. The only air conditioning on the ship was in those spaces with critical equipment. Other spaces, such as crew berthing and mess desks, went without.

The heat and sandy grime continually grated on the crew. Everyone, except those who worked in air conditioned spaces, was absolutely miserable.

Before the ship departed from San Diego, I had come up with a secret plan that I hoped would help break some of the tension of life at sea for weeks on end under harsh conditions. After about two weeks of sweltering heat in the Arabian Sea, I asked the XO for permission for the MAs switch to civilian clothes in which they would serve iced tea to the crew. Giving me that look that said, "You are as crazy as a loon," the XO got the required permission from the captain. I asked for permission to use the 1MC and with permission, passed the word throughout the ship to "Execute Operation Penguin." Of course the crew had no idea what Operation Penguin was.

When the idea first surfaced in San Diego, some of the ship's master-at arms had been reluctant to bring tuxedos or dark suits, white shirts, and black bow ties aboard. Although some of the men were looking forward to the prank, other MAs remained reticent.

But when Operation Penguin was called, they quickly switched to suits and tuxedos, and served iced tea to the crew, both inside and outside of the skin of the ship. A chime was used to announce tea service on the 1MC saying, "1600, tea will now be served."

Of course the crew thought it was crazy, but they loved it, and they repeatedly asked when we would do it again.

About a week later, when steak and lobster were on the dinner menu, (that only happened once or twice during a six-month deployment), I obtained permission to use the ship's silver. Now the ship's silver included silver platters, goblets, pitchers, and other ornate utensils provided as a gift by the City of Chicago when the ship was first commissioned. The silver settings were considered sacred. They were normally kept in a glass encased display case in the officer's ward room. Most of the enlisted men didn't even know that the silver existed. Once again, the XO rolled his eyes at the unusual request. He was good at that.

Porcelain dinnerware was only used in the officer's ward room and in the captain and admiral's mess, never in the enlisted mess where metal trays were used. A single table was set up in the enlisted after mess decks with four porcelain and real silver place settings complete with trays, platters, and candelabra from the ward room display case. Stanchions with decorative rope surrounded the lone table, isolating it from passageways leading to sculleries. Word quickly got around that the admiral and the captain were going to have dinner in the enlisted mess. No one, not even the cooks, knew for sure what was about to happen.

Chow call was passed over the 1MC as it was each evening at that hour. Several hundred crewmen who were not on watch lined the two main passageways stretching nearly the entire length of the ship. Two ship's master-at-arms dressed in normal dungaree uniforms made their way down the line of waiting crewmen, selecting a total of four men of differing ethnicity. The four men were randomly chosen, the only requirement being that no two men could be from the same department.

Ironically, none of the four selectees had a sterling record on the ship. They were not told what was about to happen. Rather, they were only told to follow the master-at-arms. Clearly, the four selectees were worried. Being singled out by the ship's sheriffs could not be a good thing.

When they arrived on the after mess decks, they found four tuxedo-clad MAs and a Maître d' waiting to seat them at the ornate table. The rumor went around that this was to be their last supper and that I was going to shoot them after dinner. Oh, the power of rumors! The four men were noticeably worried.

Each of the four selectees had his own tuxedo-clad server who tossed individually made-to-order salads, mixed with a salad dressing of their personal choice. Steak and lobster were cooked to individual taste and served on porcelain plates placed with white- gloved hands on silver platters. Since alcoholic beverages are not allowed on U. S. Navy vessels, a chilled soft drink was splashed gingerly around a single decoratively cut cube of ice and served in an exquisite wine glass. A selection of desserts were offered and served followed by cigars, which the four men were allowed to light and smoke on the after mess deck – a real departure from ship's policy.

By the time dessert was served, other crewmen who had finished their meals were lining up to drop off their trays in the scullery. They crowded around the roped-off area and shouted to the four royal diners. The four men got into character saying, "We don't have time to talk with riff raff."

Many of the crew hurried to get their cameras to record the unusual event on film. Operation Penguin was a huge success.

Chapter 2.8 Mombasa in Kenya, Africa

(August 1974)

After a month at sea in sweltering heat and grit, the Chicago anchored on the 9th of August in the middle of a Mombasa sea channel in Kenya, Africa. Many of the ship's black sailors were greatly anticipating the visit to Mombasa, which they considered as the gateway to their ancestral roots. They were devastated when they went ashore and flashed their "black power" raised fists only to find that black Africans weren't at all impressed with dashiki-clad black Americans. The Africans, who were dressed in conservative, well-pressed trousers, and starched long-sleeved white shirts, were more interested in making a living. The experience quieted the ship's black community for quite a while. It seemed to be a real learning experience.

Because the ship had anchored in the channel instead of at a pier, personnel going ashore had to make the trip on liberty boats. Most of the crew was ashore. I stood on deck, getting my first look at Mombasa, when I noticed a huge sign on the beach that said, "Sharks, no swimming." As if on cue, a shark, maybe twenty feet in length swam lazily by the ship. Okay, no swimming in Mombasa!

Chapter 2.9 The Island of Rodrigues

On August 21st, the Chicago took officials, including the U.S. Ambassador, from the Republic of Mauritius, on a two-day cruise to the island of Rodrigues. Because the island's population was so small, only a select few officers and senior enlisted personnel got the opportunity to go ashore. Gold Badge went ashore while I stayed on the ship.

The silhouette of the Island looked like an early 1900's movie depiction of a penal colony. The island was small, and the horizon barely rose above the high tide mark. There were no trees or hills that I could see from the deck of the ship. The channel from the ship to the populated part of the island was so treacherous that only the island's experienced boat handlers could navigate the entrance through the reef. Liberty boats remained cradled on the ship while a small fleet of islander's ferried the hand-picked crew members and officials to the island.

Earlier in the day, as the ship was steaming toward the island, the ambassador received an urgent plea for medical assistance for a young girl. Apparently, a boulder had fallen and had crushed her leg. She would die if the leg wasn't amputated, and there was no surgeon on the island. The Chicago's medical doctor was a surgeon, and at the urging of the State Department and the ambassador, the captain and the admiral gave permission for him to perform the surgery at the island's hospital. The operation was successful, and the girl's life was saved.

The townspeople so appreciated the lifesaving surgery that they collectively broke out a local brew; a wine made by individual families. There were no bars or restaurants, so the celebration was carried out on a grassy common in the center of town. The locally-made wine packed quite a punch. And the local brew wasn't the only punches being served.

After drinking for an hour or so, fistfights broke out among the crew. So many fights broke out, that the captain curtailed liberty. Gold Badge and the few sailors and officers who had remained somewhat sober, herded the drunken sailors to the embarkation point to board boats for the trip back to the ship. The so-called "best behaved" crewmen fought on the common, they fought in the staging area, a few fought in the boats, and some even tried to continue the fistfights on the ship.

The chief engineer tried to punch out the XO on the quarterdeck. The XO tried to take over the responsibilities of the Officer of the Deck, giving orders for handling the returning crew. It fell to me to tell the XO to go to bed. I went so far as to post a guard on the XO's door to ensure that he didn't go wandering around the ship, more for his safety than for other crew members. Similarly, the chief engineer was escorted to his stateroom.

A couple of crewmen ended up in sick bay, much to the consternation of the Medical Department's corpsmen who were required to establish watches to ensure that the drunken crewmen didn't go into convulsions as a result of the alcohol that they had consumed. Two other fighting crewmen were placed in the brig for their safety, which of course upset the Marines who had to initiate watches to make sure the drunken crewmen didn't try to commit suicide in the brig. That must have been some very powerful brew.

The next morning, as sea detail was being set, the XO looked at me sheepishly and asked, "Did you really order me to go to bed last night?"

"Oh, no, sir," I said, "but I did strongly suggest it." The XO rolled his eyes and said, "Oh, that hurts."

The ship got underway and returned the official visitors to Mauritius, then headed back out to sea to make a port call in Singapore before heading back to Subic Bay.

Chapter 2.10 The Hong Kong Incident

(October 1974)

In October, the ship had a port call in Hong Kong. The night before arrival, I was summoned to the admiral's cabin. The admiral explained that he had received a warning message stating that for the past couple of years, several sailors and Marines who had been assigned to naval vessels visiting Hong Kong died after drinking at local bars. The cause of their deaths was unknown. Both the admiral and the captain, after reading the warning, wanted to ensure that nothing like that happened to anyone on the Chicago. The admiral ordered me to conduct an investigation to determine why military deaths had occurred in Hong Kong.

"Sir," I said as respectfully as I could, "I have no authority to conduct criminal investigations in foreign ports. That's the responsibility of NIS."

The admiral yelled, "Are you refusing to obey my orders?"

"No sir. I'm just informing you that I have no jurisdiction ashore."

"Damn it," the admiral shouted, "I don't care who has jurisdiction. Just go out there and find out what's killing our sailors and Marines."

"Aye aye, sir" I said, as I beat a hasty retreat.

I called a meeting of the ship's master-at-arms for the purpose of conjuring up a strategy to determine why and how U.S. sailors and Marines were being targeted at local bars. They decided that I would be the bait, and two other MAs would constantly watch my back. As far as the MAs were concerned, this would be a wasted liberty. They didn't believe for a second that we might be successful.

Based on the message, deaths occurred at three different bars. It would have been easy to place those three bars off limits however, experience dictates that if you place an establishment "off limits," that's where the crew will eventually end up. Since the deaths occurred so infrequently and since there was nothing known as to why the deaths had occurred, placing the establishments off limits would have created a mini-international incident. Bar owners didn't like losing money because their places of business were placed off limits.

I wasn't much of a drinker: I could make one or two beers last all night. Our team was in the second bar, having found nothing after two hours in the first bar. I was nursing my first beer when one of the MAs watching my back uttered the prearranged duress code. I froze until my backup could resolve the problem.

The backup team grabbed the bar girl saying that she had slipped something into my drink. The drink was placed in a plastic evidence bag and the girl was ushered into a booth for questioning. The bartender threatened to call the police.

"Call the police, we could use their help," I said.

That was a bluff. We didn't want to get involved with the police or anybody else. But the bartender didn't reach for the phone.

Meanwhile, the team told the bar girl that they were investigating a murder, and that she would not be turned over to the police unless she lied. She was noticeably scared.

According to the bar girl, military personnel no longer spent money the way they used to before the fall of Viet Nam. So the owners resorted to theft by giving the girls pills to be placed in the drinks of those people who were not spending freely. The girls had been told that the pills were "Mickey Finns" which would only knock out the patron so that the barman could steal their wallets and valuables. The drugged patron would then be dragged into the alley behind the bar until he woke up. But a few of the drugged patrons didn't wake up.

Whimpering, the bar girl reluctantly surrendered the few pills that she had. The whole procedure only took a few minutes. However, we could see that the bartender was getting increasingly nervous. He threatened to call his bosses. Now the team might be able to deal with the police, but bar owners would be a different situation. The team left with the pills and the drink, and returned to the ship.

With the help of the ship's medical staff, the MAs were able to identify the pills as an anticoagulant that could, under the right conditions, cause blood vessels to burst, causing the drunken victim to strangle on his own blood. I reported the findings to the captain and the admiral, both of whom decided that they needed to send a message regarding the findings to every command in the western Pacific and to the Pentagon.

It was ironic! It was only because I wasn't drinking that the bar girl felt compelled to slip the pill into my drink. Had I been a big spender and a heavy drinker, the team would never have discovered why the deaths had occurred, or what caused them. After reporting to the admiral and the captain, I went to my bunk for a night's sleep.

Within a couple of hours, I was awakened by the Messenger of the Watch who said that I was to report to the admiral's cabin. When I got to the cabin, the captain handed me a message from the Naval Investigative Service demanding that I be placed in the ship's brig pending a Court Martial for conducting an investigation in a foreign jurisdiction without authority and for disrupting a two-year investigation that the NIS/NCIS had been conducting for the same purpose.

I saw my naval career ending while spending the next few years in a federal prison. Evidently both the captain and the admiral just wanted me to read the message. I wasn't placed in the brig, and I never heard anything more about a Court Martial. After being excused, I went to the mess decks for breakfast. It had been a long night and I was still beat, but I needed to eat and build up some energy. The message had really set me on edge.

I hadn't even finished breakfast when I was called to the captain's cabin. Evidently the ship's message regarding the pills had been redirected to both military and civilian agencies. I was to be temporarily assigned to the British Royal Military Police, Special Investigations Branch, to assist in the investigation of local drug rings that were believed to be selling drugs to visiting military personnel.

Over the next two days, the Royal Military Police Investigations identified three drug rings; two Chinese and one Coast Guard. By then, I had worked day and night for three days. It was 0500 on the third day when I finally returned to the ship for some much needed sleep.

At about 0900, the Messenger of the Watch woke me and said that I was to report to the captain's cabin. I got dressed, splashed some cold water on face, combed my hair and reported to the captain who directed me to change into a summer white uniform and report to the office of the British Governor of Hong Kong. A lorry would pick me up to take me the governor's office.

I quickly shaved and showered, changed into the appropriate uniform, and met the British driver who took me to the governor's office. I was directed to a waiting room with deep leather couches where I almost immediately fell sound asleep. I didn't wake until about 1700. When I awoke, I was fully stretched out on the couch and no one else was in the waiting room. Looking out of the window, I noticed that it was just starting to get dark. A door adjacent to the waiting area was open and light emanated from a desk lamp. The governor was working at his desk.

My crisp white uniform looked as if it had been slept in, which of course it had. I apologized for my appearance, but the governor just laughed while he poured coffee for the two of us. I was surprised that he wasn't drinking tea. We sipped hot black coffee and talked about the investigations that had been conducted by the Royal Military Police.

The governor had assured the admiral that the investigations would continue after the Chicago left Hong Kong, but he also wanted to invite me to a weekend of rest and relaxation at the governor's mansion. The governor assured me that both the admiral and the captain had approved. But alas, it was not to be.

A typhoon was bearing down on Hong Kong and the ship would be putting to sea to ride out the storm. Ship's personnel were being recalled and I felt it was my duty to sail with the ship. After the ship got underway, the executive officer saw me and asked what I was doing aboard. I answered that barring instructions to the contrary, I thought it was my duty to sail with the ship. The XO laughed saying that he didn't expect me to return to the ship, especially since the ship would return to port after the typhoon had passed. I never did get another opportunity to visit with the governor or to stay in the governor's mansion. But I did finally get a full night's sleep, even with a storm raging outside.

After the typhoon had passed, the Chicago returned to Hong Kong to refuel and to take on provisions for continued operations at sea and for the trip back to Subic Bay. Those masters-at-arms who were not on duty were invited by the British Royal Military Police, Special Investigative Branch, to a very special dinner.

Chapter 2.11 A Very Special Dinner

(October 1974)

On the street level, the building housed a public restaurant. The second floor contained a semi-private restaurant. But the third floor had a dining area only for the invited. Few people, even those who lived in Hong Kong, ever got an invitation.

The private restaurant contained a gymnasium-sized room with four large round tables. Each table could seat twelve to fifteen people. There was a large Broadway-style stage on the side of the room opposite from the entrance. A maître d' was assigned to each table, and each person at the table had his own server. If you took a sip of water, the glass of water was removed the instant you placed it back on the table and a new full glass of water appeared.

The center of the table contained a large lazy Susan where a variety of the foods were placed. We sampled food from each dish. The Broadway-sized stage was soon filled with acts from all over the world. It was truly a glorious evening.

And when the evening ended, the maître d' handed me the bill – a bill for about one thousand dollars per person. I almost had heart failure. And I was embarrassed because I probably had about twenty dollars. The other petty officers were faced with the same dilemma. Our British host laughed and took the bill. He just wanted us to understand and appreciate how special the dinner was. He ended the evening by presenting us with their unit tie. Although we could not have a tie that said "Royal Military Police," we were given ties that said "Friend of the Royal Military Police" in Chinese symbols. I still wear my tie on rare occasions.

Chapter 2.12 The USS Chicago Tiger Cruise

(December 1974)

Males from ages 11 to 60 (Tigers) who were related to members of the crew and who were in good physical condition could ride the ship from Hawaii to San Diego. Females were not allowed, which was a source of great consternation for the executive officer because he had three daughters who desperately wanted to go on the Tiger Cruise. They reportedly wrote to the Chief of Naval Operations asking for a waiver to no avail. My oldest son, Jim, made the trip.

I didn't have the money to take Jim to the hotels on Waikiki where guests were having luaus, but we walked along the beach behind the hotels and watched others partying. We had a significantly less expensive dinner at a restaurant in town and looked through some of the local shops. The next morning, the ship got underway. Jim got seasick and he remained seasick for the first twenty-four hours, so he missed many of the first day's activities at sea.

Each department was required to have activities for the Tigers. The Marines broke out machine guns on the fantail, closely supervising and assisting each Tiger as they fired the weapons. That was one of the favorite activities for both the younger and the older Tigers. One night at sea, the Marines and the Weapons Department put on a combined firefight demonstration using different types of weapons. The fireworks were dramatic in the night sky, but to me, they were equally ominous.

There was very little inactive time for Tigers. Every minute of the day and night was planned. So by the third or fourth day at sea, it wasn't unusual for some of the Tigers, young and old, to sneak off to their bunks for an afternoon nap.

There were several places on the ship that required either a secret or top secret clearance in order to gain entry. I had a secret clearance, but that wasn't sufficient to enter missile spaces. So you can imagine how surprised I was to learn that the admiral had personally escorted the Tigers through some of the missile spaces. Jim actually got to see parts of the ship that I didn't see in the three years I was assigned to the ship. I couldn't enter missile spaces, even in a law enforcement capacity. That policy later came back to haunt me.

Simultaneous with the Tiger Cruise, and in order to reduce the time necessary to clear Customs upon arrival in the United States, the U.S. Customs Service deployed a couple of Customs Officers to ride the ship from Hawaii to San Diego for the purpose of co-ordinating the search for contraband throughout the vessel. The Health Department sent representatives to inspect the ship to ensure that we were not bringing anything, including food products, which might cause a threat to the health of the general public. All this was to be done before anybody could board or leave the ship in San Diego.

Searching a ship for contraband is impossible. It can't be done in five days on a ship the size of a cruiser. To help conduct the mandatory search, every department's chiefs, officers, and senior petty officers were arranged into teams to search work spaces and the lockers of the crew.

A lot depends on the attitude of the captain and the executive officer. If they view the search as an imposition, then that attitude permeates the crew and affects the search teams, so very little actual searching gets done. In the end, the customs officers decide whether the crew has done an effective job. Basically, the goal is to convince the customs officers that the search was successful so that they will sign the release papers allowing the crew to disembark.

On the fifth day of the Tiger Cruise, (December 14, 1974), we arrived at our homeport in San Diego. Wives, friends, and families were on the pier. They had been there for several hours. Tying up a ship to a pier, especially one as large as the USS Chicago and clearing U.S. Customs and Health Services takes quite a while. So the Tigers stood on deck waving to family members ashore. Jim had something white on his right forearm that looked suspiciously like a cast. My wife Pat became alarmed. However, the cast was just a product of one of the activities that the Medical Department had provided for the Tigers. The cast was actually two halves taped together with white tape. When she realized that she had been the victim of a prank, she swatted him. Then she swatted me too. Welcome home, sailor!

Chapter 2.13 You Can't Win Them All

(December 1974)

Three days after returning to San Diego, I received a nighttime phone call from the ship's duty master-at-arms. Apparently the

Coronado Police had arrested one of the *Chicago's* crew who was in possession of about three pounds of hashish. Three pounds of hashish in San Diego would be worth several thousands of dollars on the street.

During interrogation, the suspect told police that another *Chicago* sailor had smuggled about 30 pounds of hashish in Karachi, where it lay hidden in the missile spaces. The smugglers decided to wait a couple of nights before retrieving the hashish because there would be fewer people and less activity on the ship.

According to the arrested sailor, the ringleader was a missile technician with an impeccable record. The technician's enlistment was set to expire, and he would be leaving the Navy within a couple of months. The case was turned over to NIS, and the sailor who was in the custody of the Coronado Police agreed to testify against the ringleader.

Within weeks, the ringleader was formally charged and taken to Court Martial where he was found guilty, based primarily on the testimony of his shipmate.

He was to be removed from the Navy with a Bad Conduct Discharge, and sentenced to prison.

The ringleader's father took out a second mortgage on his home, hired civilian attorneys, and took the case to the Court of Appeals. The Appeals judge ruled that a co-conspirator's testimony could not be used, thereby overturning the conviction. The decision of the court being final, the ringleader was freed. He was processed out of the Navy with a Honorable Discharge, and the Navy had to pay him back pay and allowances for the time that he was held (pending and during his trial) following the expiration of his enlistment.

As he was leaving the ship for the last time, the ringleader leaned over and whispered in my ear saying, "I beat you. I have over $60,000 and you don't have a dime." I told him that I felt sorry for his father who one day would learn that his son was a drug dealer. He laughed and left the ship and the Navy. All too often, crime does pay – even in the Navy!

Chapter 2.14 War Games

(March 1975)

When major repairs had been completed, the ship and its crew participated in Exercise Valiant Heritage. That was a big deal because the exercise included ships from England, Canada, New Zealand, and a carrier task force from the United States, all of which were the good guys. The *USS Chicago* and a few destroyers were the bad guys.

Since the ships and aircraft couldn't actually shoot at each other, a system was devised in which a neutral team of judges would roll the dice to determine how much damage was done to each ship after a skirmish. Realism was not part of the scenario, at least not when applied to the bad guys.

The captain and the officers of the *USS Chicago* proved themselves to be near geniuses in their ability to make the ship show up where it wasn't expected. Over the course of the first few days, the *Chicago* darted from one place to another along the western coast of the United States, placing well aimed missile shots on target, and eliminating from play many of the ships that belonged to the good guys. The Orange Force (the bad guys) lost their destroyers, but the Mighty Chi kept moving, kept shooting, and kept winning battles at sea.

Finally, after nearly a week of running and shooting, our CO decided to go after the good guy's carrier, which was located off the coast of San Diego. But the *Chicago* was near San Francisco, and the good guys had a screen of ships off of Los Angeles and Long Beach, just waiting to pounce on our lone cruiser.

The CO took a page out of a novel. He wanted to make a speed run until the ship approached the screen, and then he wanted to use deception to ease by the enemy warships in the dead of night. I was to do whatever I could to make the *USS Chicago* look and sound like a cruise ship. Time to break out the bands again!

The deck department installed lights along the starboard side of the ship to simulate portholes. Then they put up Christmas lights to look like the party lights commonly used on cruise ships. The band assembled on the fantail. Several of the crew, getting into the spirit of the deception, cut the heads off of mops and wore them on their heads to simulate long hair. They also fabricated dresses out of canvas, butcher paper, and other materials. Any light that could distinguish the *Chicago* as a warship was extinguished. *Chicago* was slowed to cruise ship speed, staying within those sea lanes normally traveled by cruise ships. It was well after midnight when we passed through the screen of enemy warships. About thirty crewmen in civilian clothes and make-shift dresses had paired up and were dancing on the fantail as the band blared loudly.

The ruse was successful. At dawn, the *Chicago* attacked the carrier, placing a nuclear warhead inside one of its hangar bays.

No one expected the *Chicago* to show up in the San Diego area. Technically, the time it would take for such a trip was beyond the ship's capability. But somehow, the engineers had given the captain the speed he needed. After shooting and hitting the carrier with a nuclear missile, the captain headed out to sea, away from the coast, to await the decision of the judges as to whether the exercise would be terminated. No one on the *Chicago* could have anticipated the roll of the dice.

According to the judges, the nuclear missile had only *knocked out the carrier's ice cream machine*. Come on! A strike by a nuclear warhead can only destroy an ice cream machine?

Eventually, the *Chicago* was attacked by the carrier's aircraft and the task force submarines and the exercise was declared "finished." Not won or lost; just finished. But the admiral who was running the exercise decided that he wanted to return to San Diego with the *Chicago* instead of with the carrier. It was the thirty-two knots that had allowed the *Chicago* to show up where it was not expected time after time. The rated top speed of the *Chicago* was something less. The captain got on the 1MC and praised the crew for their achievements. Then he said, "I don't think anyone believed that the bad guys could actually win."

The crew had once again proven that the USS Chicago really was, at that time, the "World's Most Powerful Warship." Also, the *Chicago's* near win probably scared the hell out of Pentagon planners. Well done, Chi-town!

Chapter 2.15 WESTPAC II

Between war games and repairs, the year flew by. On April 13, 1976, the ship again deployed to the western Pacific. This time we sailed with an amphibious group and conducted multi-ship exercises enroute to Yokosuka, Japan. We arrived in May.

One young sailor, who had married before leaving San Diego, was met by his bride in Hawaii, Guam, and Japan. She returned to the states when the ship left for the Philippines in early July. The ship participated in numerous exercises, returning to Subic Bay in mid-August for two weeks of repairs before sailing for Hong Kong. One evening, I was called to the captain's cabin. Apparently the newlywed had been enjoying the charms of a local Pilipino bar girl who decided that he was the man for her.

She had filed civil charges with the Philippine government indicating that he had played with her affections and that she was going to have his child. The Philippine government asked the captain to surrender the sailor. The captain refused. The local police stationed a police officer at the bottom of the brow for the purpose of apprehending the sailor when he stepped off the ship.

Filing paternity charges was a common ploy in Olongapo, the city outside the naval base at Subic Bay. A bar girl would file charges saying that she was pregnant. The sailor would be arrested, then after paying the girl several thousand dollars, the girl would release her legal hold on the sailor. Usually, the girl suddenly wasn't pregnant. It was typically a bar girl scam. Of course sometimes, the girl really was pregnant. The newlywed didn't have thousands of dollars, and his shipmates in his division couldn't come up with that much money either. The captain wanted me to figure out how to get the newlywed back to the states without his being arrested by the Olongapo Police.

About twenty-five midshipmen from the U.S. Naval Academy had deployed with the Chicago on a training cruise. They were scheduled to go back to the states in two days on an aircraft that would take off from Cubi Point, just across the bay. The problem was how to get the newlywed to Cubi Point without the knowledge of the local police. A Midshipman of about the same height and weight as the newlywed volunteered to stay on the Chicago for the rest of the cruise, thus allowing the newlywed to take his place on the plane. Permission was granted by the powers that be.

The newlywed dressed in the midshipman's uniform. The Personnel Officer gave him a new identification card with the midshipman's name but with the newlywed's photo, and new orders allowing him to return to North Island until the ship returned from its deployment.

The policeman, who was located at the end of the brow, carefully scrutinized the identification of every person leaving the ship, but he did not recognize the accused. That was not the only time that I would be asked to spirit a serviceman away from a host country's jurisdiction.

The ship sailed for Hong Kong where we spent six days before joining the *USS Enterprise* (CVN-65) for more war-games. After the exercises, the ship sailed back to Subic Bay for repairs, and finally in September, we headed home.

By then I was a first class petty officer nearing the end of my tour on the *USS Chicago*, and I was due for shore duty. My wife Pat and I wanted to stay in the San Diego area, but my detailer wanted to send me elsewhere. There was still time to see if a San Diego billet might develop before I had to leave the *Chicago*. So without committing to any of the assignments that the detailer currently needed to fill, I decided to wait for a few months before calling the detailer again.

Chapter 2.16 Slapping a Three Star Admiral

(December 1976)

The ship had just been tied to the pier at NAS North Island. A number of senior officers were visiting the ship. As a retired three star admiral entered the athwartship[13] passageway from the quarterdeck, I brought up my right hand in a snappy salute. The retired admiral walked into the path of my rising hand, the force of which knocked him into the bulkhead. The old admiral's eyes were glazed and he was noticeably wobbly as he walked to the captain's cabin steadied by a couple of junior officers.

The XO, who was the last in the line of the official party, rolled his eyes as he passed me. I wondered whether smacking the admiral was

---

13 Athwartship means across the ship

some kind of reverse karma for getting punched out by the command-ing officer.

Chapter 2.17 Assignment to the Presidential Yacht

(March 1977)

Several months had passed since I had talked to my detailer about a shore duty billet in San Diego. One day while the ship was in port, I was called to the captain's cabin where the CO introduced me to a Navy captain who had flown in from Washington, D.C. to interview me for duty on the presidential yacht, the *USS Sequoia* (AG-23).

The admiral, who had served as Task Force 75 Commander dur-ing the May 1974 WESPAC cruise, had gone on to become the Chief of Naval Personnel. It was he who had nominated me for the chief master-at-arms (CMAA) billet on the yacht, where I would get to work antiterrorism cases with the Secret Service.

Following the interview, the D.C. captain told me that I would have to shave off my mustache and get a "high and tight" haircut like the Marines wear. He then asked me if I would accept the CMAA billet on the presidential yacht. I said that I would give him an answer after I had the opportunity to talk with my wife. The D.C. captain gave me his telephone number in Washington, and then directed me to call him with my answer by the end of the week.

My wife, Pat, and I talked most of the night about duty on the presi-dential yacht, and also about the increased cost of living that a move to the Washington D.C. area represented. We were almost getting by finan-cially in San Diego, but not quite. Living in the Washington area meant a 20 percent or more increase in the cost of living with no increase in pay. The next day, I made the required phone call and declined the honor.

Two days later, the captain from D.C. called to "convince me to accept the orders to the presidential yacht." Again I declined. The captain asked. "What would it take for you to accept the orders?"

I said that I firmly believed that President Carter was going to sell the yacht, but I would accept the orders only if someone in the president's office assured me that the yacht would not be sold.

USS Sequoia (AG-23)
The Presidential Yacht (U.S. Navy Photo)

Another two days went by and the D.C. captain again appeared on the Chicago. To say the least, he was extremely upset at having to travel from coast to coast just because of some first class petty officer.

Again, I found myself in the captain's cabin where I was told to sit. There was no conversation, no coffee was served, and no pleasantry offered or given. The D.C. captain stared at me as if I was some kind of a venomous snake. After about ten long and silent minutes, the phone rang. It was the White House calling. The CO handed me the phone.

The Commanding Officer of the *USS Sequoia* had been directed to call me from the White House and to assure me that the president was not going to sell the yacht. He did as he was told. True to my word, I accepted the assignment and was immediately handed a set of written orders.

It would be several months before I could report to Washington D.C. and the presidential yacht. First, I was temporarily transferred to the Police Department at the Naval Amphibious Base in Coronado. While I was there, I was subjected to an intense background investigation by the FBI and the Secret Service. I went home and told Pat to get ready to move to Washington. She wasn't all that happy about the move, but we were both excited about the assignment as chief master-at-arms on the presidential yacht.

(April 2, 1977)

It was Saturday and I was looking forward to having a day off. I sat on the couch with the first hot cup of coffee of the day. I opened the *San Diego Union Tribune*. The first thing I noticed was a picture of the Sequoia, and the caption, "President To Give Up Yacht." A short two-column story on a back page (page A-2) said it all: "President Will Sell Yacht." That left me with orders to Washington D.C., but where in Washington?

I wouldn't be able to get through to the detailer until Monday at the earliest, so I spent the rest of the weekend worrying about what was to become of my family and me.

I started calling the detailer at 0600 San Diego time on Monday. Where previously the detailer, a Master Chief MA, couldn't do enough for me, now that the yacht was to be sold, he wouldn't even return my phone calls. The admiral, however, did eventually return my call, saying that he still thought it would be a good career move for me to accept a billet in Washington. I truthfully answered that we couldn't financially afford to be assigned to the D.C. area. After a half hour on the phone, the admiral finally relented and within a few days, new orders were cut reassigning me to Naval Station San Diego.

What I didn't know was that the admiral had also called the Commanding Officer at Naval Station San Diego, so when I did arrive at my new assignment, I was unprepared for my reception.

CHAPTER THREE

Chapter 3.1 Naval Station San Diego

(October 1977)

I reported to the naval station and was told that the commanding officer wanted to see me. That was unusual. Captains of very large installations, like Naval Station San Diego, don't usually take the time to meet with petty officers who were reporting for duty. Never before had I met the captain. The CO's secretary assured me that I was expected, and that she had specific orders to fit me into the captain's schedule when I arrived. I waited.

"You don't look like Superman," the captain said as he shook my hand.

"I beg your pardon, sir?" I replied.

The captain grinned and told me about a telephone conversation he had with the Chief of Naval Personnel, who had left him with the impression that Superman would be reporting to the naval station for duty. I assured him that I wasn't Superman.

"I want you to clean up the barracks," said the Captain.

I was devastated. I was a law enforcement petty officer and the captain wanted to put me in charge of cleaning the barracks?

"No, I want you to clean up the criminal activity and vandalism that's going on in the barracks."

The barracks consisted of five three-story buildings. Each room housed between two and four sailors.

Use of narcotics and other drugs, vandalism, and theft was rampant because there was no supervision. I would be part of the police department, but my area of responsibility would be the barracks.

Vandalism and theft are often the symptoms of the use of drugs. So the root cause was most likely drugs. That's what I decided to tackle first. I talked with the civilian Chief of Police who wasn't happy to have a first class petty officer on his police force who could talk directly to the commanding officer. The chief agreed to provide more police patrols in the barracks area, what today would be called saturated patrol. When police officers, military and civilian, weren't on other assignments, they were required to drive through the parking lots, and as time allowed, get out of their police cars and walk through the public areas of the barracks. Suddenly, the barracks weren't the haven from the police that they had been.

There were some complaints about the increased police presence, but for the most part, sailors were happy to see that the commanding officer was finally taking an interest in the unlawful activities that were going on in the barracks.

Naval Station San Diego had never previously used drug detection dog teams in the barracks. And because the naval station had no drug dogs, arrangements for canine assistance had to be made with other naval installations in the area. The closest facility with a drug detection dog team was the Antisubmarine Warfare (ASW) School at Point Loma. I notified the naval station commanding officer that I intended to extensively use drug detection dog teams in the barracks. The CO approved.

Drug detection dog use is a team effort. The dogs only point to where drugs are suspected to be; for instance, in a locked closet or locker. The police can't enter the locker because there is a presumption of privacy. Therefore, they must either get permission from the owner or person assigned to the locker, or they must explain in writing why they believe that there are drugs in a particular area. That means they would have to verify how many times the drug detection dog had been successful in finding drugs, and how many false positives the dog had made. If the commanding officer grants a search warrant, then police personnel must conduct a search of the specific area that the dog pointed to, usually in the presence of the person assigned to the room and locker.

The naval station barracks were constructed in a manner that was similar to a Holiday Inn. That is, there was a small common area leading to four rooms. The first room that the drug detection dog checked resulted in a response to a locker. The police then had to identify who was assigned to that particular locker, present the request for a search warrant to the commanding officer, get that person from his or her assigned job somewhere on the naval station, serve them with the search warrant, escort them to the room being searched, and conduct the search. When drugs were found, police had to identify, collect, and preserve the evidence for use in court. The suspect was advised of his Miranda rights and was interrogated as to his or her sources for the drugs. In short, a single hit could result in literally hours of work for the police.

The dog handler usually continued checking rooms well ahead of station police. The barracks manager opened each room so that the dog team could conduct the inspection. The manager waited outside the room. If the dog alerted, the handler noted the location, which would be provided in writing to the search team. The room's lock core was changed to ensure that no one could enter and remove evidence before the search team conducted the required search.

The dog alerted so many times in the second room that the police spent an entire eight hour shift searching that one room. All four of the residents were involved. The drug dog team got so far ahead of the investigators that the police had to send him home.

The use of military working dog teams in the barracks caused quite a ruckus among the residents. But the results of just two rooms had been so overwhelming that the captain told the residents that drug dog teams would be used every week, daily if necessary.

Sailors weren't required to live in the barracks. The barracks were a low cost way of housing unmarried sailors, and those married sailors whose families lived out of the area. Sailors who were dealing drugs to supplement their incomes eventually moved out. They could afford to live in an apartment in San Diego.

Chapter 3.2 The Chief's Initiation

(October 1977)

Prior to reporting to the naval station, I had taken the test for E-7 and was selected for advancement to Chief Petty Officer (CPO). In other military services, making E-7 is just another step in the chain of advancement. In the Navy, making chief is a really big deal. For one thing, the enlisted man or woman making chief gets to wear officer-style uniforms rather than bell bottoms. A Navy chief's status has no equal in other services, except maybe the Coast Guard. Being a Navy chief is commonly referred to as being the next thing to a god. In the Navy, the commanding officer is a god.

Making chief also meant undergoing the chief's initiation. Each chief candidate had a sponsor. My sponsor was then Senior Chief (now Master Chief Retired) Frank Durazo, the naval station's Assistant Chief of Police. At three in the morning on initiation day, a naval station police officer who was a chief petty officer and a civilian naval station police officer arrived in a marked police car at my residence in Santee, a bedroom community located east of the city of San Diego.

The family German shepherd started barking, which woke me from a deep sleep. I answered the door, and the police officers announced that they were there to pick me up for my initiation. I invited them in and asked them to be seated in the living room while I dressed. They made a tactical error, one that every police rookie is taught not to make. They sat next to each other on the couch. I told them not to move or the dog would bite them. Then I told the dog to "watch em." The dog's ears sprang up and she sat facing the two police officers, watching them intently. Every time they moved even a little bit, she growled a low-pitched menacing growl.

I said, "Well guys, I'm going back to bed, see you in a couple of hours."

I went to bed, but I could hear the chief saying, "Come on, John. You know we have to do this."

Pat and I giggled under the covers. The tables had been turned, and they were not very comfortable with their predicament. The two police officers knew that the senior chief would give them hell for being so easily trapped.

Finally, I got up, got dressed in my new chief's uniform (without insignia), and went with them to the naval station to start my initiation – in a jail cell.

The purpose of the chief's initiation was to prove to the chief petty officer candidate that he or she could suffer the slings and arrows of humiliation without being permanently scarred. Actually, the initiation was fun as long as the chiefs didn't get carried away. One drunken chief did get carried away and I almost decked him, but my sponsor and the other police department chiefs interceded and saved me from embarrassment and from an even harder initiation. The chiefs' community was very tight, much tighter than the officers' community.

The antics and rites associated with a chief's initiation, especially one that took place years ago, cannot be revealed herein. However, due to the objections of people who, over many years, took exception with the chief's initiation, the process has significantly changed. Today's

CPO-initiate suffers very little or none of the hazing that used to take place in years past. Following the initiation, I was a chief – "tested, selected, and initiated." It was a big deal.

Chapter 3.3 Busting the Drug Detection Dog Handler

(March 1978)

We continued inspecting rooms using drug dog teams. In fact, I went to Naval Air Station Miramar to schedule the use of their dogs in addition to the dog team from the ASW School. Eventually, we got through the entire barracks complex and started again. We mixed up the order of inspections so that no one knew in advance which rooms would be inspected. We still got some complaints about using the detection dog teams, but not very many. I also received complaints about missing money following the inspections. Normally that is a common complaint used to cast aspersions on the dog team. I dismissed the first few complaints, but then noticed that complaints were only received after the use of the detection team from the ASW School. I decided to bait some rooms to see if cash was being taken during the inspections.

Naval station detectives placed cash, mostly twenty dollar bills, in books, clothing, and exposed wallets left on desks in four out of the sixteen rooms to be inspected. They coated the bills with a powder that was invisible to the eye, but which would show up under an ultraviolet light. None of cash was visible to anyone entering the room. That was an important aspect so that the police could not be accused of entrapment. The serial number of each bill was recorded and placed in a sealed envelope that was deposited with the station Judge Advocate General before the inspections were conducted. We did that so that no one could claim that the police had later altered the serial numbers. The inspections were conducted exactly as they always had been in the past.

When the day's inspections were completed, the ASW dog handler stopped by the office to report his progress. As the dog handler entered the office, his face and hands lit up like a Christmas tree under the ultraviolet lights that had been placed in the entryway of the office. The drug detection dog handler, himself an MA, was a thief. The police had the evidence, but the handler had an attack dog and a loaded gun.

I ordered the handler to place his dog in the bathroom. The dog handler hesitated. His eyes got big when he realized that he had been caught. Two detectives were in the office with me, so he wasn't going to get away. Again the handler was ordered to place the dog in the bathroom. Again he hesitated saying, "You caught me, didn't you?"

"Yes, now place the dog in the bathroom or I will have to shoot him," I ordered as I pulled out my gun from its holster. The handler went for his gun. The two detectives placed their hands on their guns. It was a very tense moment.

The handler placed the dog in the bathroom. The detectives disarmed him and advised him of his Miranda rights. He chose not to make a statement. The two detectives searched the handler incident to apprehension, and found all of the stolen money. They took him back to the ASW School in handcuffs. The executive officer of the ASW School was dumbfounded. I promised the XO a written report by morning, and then notified the Naval Investigative Service.

The agent said that they weren't interested in the case because it was petty theft. The agent either didn't know the NIS-mandated threshold between a misdemeanor and a felony involving the theft of cash, or he just didn't want to be bothered with another case. NIS did not assume jurisdiction. I was disappointed.

I called the military working dog handler supervisor at Naval Air Station Miramar, and explained the situation. They took custody of the drug detection dog and the ASW police canine unit (motor vehicle). It took me the rest of the day and part of the night to finish the report and to bag and tag the evidence.

At the scheduled time, the two naval station detectives and I reported to Captain's Mast at the ASW School.

I presented the case to the commanding officer, who spent the next fifteen minutes loudly berating me for apprehending his dog handler and for writing a report that contained no loopholes with which to find his dog handler-thief not guilty.

Not guilty? The detectives and I were stunned. Not only did the Captain NOT bind the thief over for Court Martial, he only gave him a sentence of thirty days restriction to the base. The ASW CO displayed substantial hostility toward the naval station police officers, and demanded that we immediately return his drug detection dog and police vehicle.

We returned to the naval station where I told the naval station commanding officer what had happened. He shook his head, saying that he could not interfere with the decisions of another commanding officer. I called and faxed a copy of the report to the MA detailer. The dog handler-thief was subsequently removed from the law enforcement rating.

Chapter 3.4 Adventures as PTA President

(January 1978 – There is life outside of the Navy)

My oldest son, Jim, was a Scout. The troop's scoutmaster quit when he was reassigned out of the area. As a former scoutmaster, I felt that I had to take over the troop or it would surely collapse. Then too, the troop's sponsor (the school's Parent, Teacher, and Student Association) couldn't find anyone to serve as president, so the sponsoring organization was in danger of collapsing too.

Without a sponsoring organization, the troop could not exist, so I became the new PTA president *and* the scoutmaster, holding both positions at the same time. The PTA met monthly at the elementary school during the work week, which meant that I would have to drive from Naval Station San Diego to the school in Santee. The meeting was usually well attended by moms. Teachers and students never attended, at least not while I was president.

The moms were used to talking for thirty or forty minutes before the formal meetings were started. I couldn't afford that kind of time. I started the meetings at the appointed hour. Meetings usually only lasted about thirty minutes because there was seldom any real business to conduct. After my year in office, *several* moms ran for PTA President. They wanted to get their meetings back to the way they had been before I took office. I was glad to give up the position, but I was equally glad that I had saved both the school's PTA and the Scout Troop.

Chapter 3.5 Scoutmaster Adventures

Every Scout troop must have a board of directors. In theory, if parents are active on the board, they will be active in the field. In practice, it didn't work that way. Board meetings, for the most part, were just another meeting that the scoutmaster had to attend. Oh, they did some good, too. They provided an avenue for boys to earn merit badges, but little else.

The one parent on whom I could rely was nicknamed Yogi, so of course he ended up being called Yogi Bear. He was the only other adult who actually went camping with the troop. The troop size varied between thirty and sixty boys, of which about twenty to forty-five Scouts went on camping trips and to summer camp; a week at the Mataguay District Scout Camp. Usually Yogi and I were the only adults who attended scout camp with the troop. Keeping track of forty-five Scouts can be a challenge for two adults, but the kids were basically well-behaved, and most of them enjoyed the camping experience.

One summer, a district commissioner called and asked me to take another troop to the Mataguay Scout Camp. Their scoutmaster was unable to take his troop, and therefore, the boys would not get to go to summer camp.

I accepted the extra assignment, especially since the district camp had prefabricated tent campsites and a mess hall where staff and Scouts ate their meals. The whole week was dedicated to activities. Several hundred Scouts from throughout the district attended camp each week in the summertime.

Chapter 3.6 Wild Fire at the District Scout Camp

One afternoon after lunch, the Scouts were sent back to their campsites while the adult staff remained behind in the mess hall to plan the rest of the day's activities. During the staff meeting, someone noticed that there was a wildfire burning down the hill toward the Scout camp. The brush and scrub oak trees were fully engulfed and the flames were being pushed toward the campsites by a brisk wind. To make matters worse, the fire had cut off the mess hall from the camp sites. There was only one road from the mess hall to the camp sites.

As a former U.S. Forest Service firefighter, I probably understood fire science better than the other adult leaders. I also understood the risk of leaving youngsters on their own as the fire converged on them in their campsites. While the rest of the leaders were trying to determine how best to handle the situation, I ran to my car and headed down the road toward the fire.

The biggest problem with driving through fire is oxygen deprivation. The fire uses up all the oxygen. Without oxygen to mix with gas, the engine stalls and the vehicle stops moving. Occupants are usually burned to death. I judged the depth of the fire crossing the road to be about thirty feet. I believed that I could get my car moving fast enough to go through the fire, even if oxygen deprivation did occur. I rolled up the windows to conserve the oxygen inside the car, backed up the car about fifty feet, placed the transmission in low gear to get the most traction and the engine's highest revolutions per minute, and drove through the fire.

I got through safely and drove to the campsites honking the car's horn to get the attention of the scouts. I ordered all the scouts to the edge of the lake, but I also ordered them not to go into the water. I didn't want a panicked scout to drown.

The boy leaders (troop leaders) carried out orders without question; they understood the gravity of the situation. They took control of their Scouts and started to count noses to ensure that they could account for all of their boys. Meanwhile, winds in the shallow canyon fanned the fire around the campsites. No one was hurt, and no tents were damaged, but some loose equipment was burned. All the scouts were accounted for, and the staff changed their operating procedures to ensure that an adult remained in camp when staff meetings were held in the mess hall. Someone took a picture of the fire and mounted it on a small plaque, which was later presented to me at a meeting of scoutmasters.

Chapter 3.7 Rain, Rain, and More Rain

About three weeks later, I took my troop to summer camp. Yogi was unable to attend, so I had the troop to myself – again. I drilled the troop in fire safety before we left Santee, but I was unprepared for what Mother Nature would throw at us.

We endured torrential rainfall for three of the six days that we were in camp. Each day, I would have to take forty-five dripping- wet sleeping bags, drive thirty miles or so to the nearest town, and dry the sleeping bags in commercial clothes dryers so that they could be used again that night.

Many of the scouting activities were cancelled and the scouts spent most of the day in their tents trying to keep the rainwater out. By the end of summer camp, I was exhausted and was more than ready to return to work.

Chapter 3.8 Murphy Canyon Navy Housing

When the rent had increased to a point that we could no longer afford to live in Santee, I applied for Navy quarters, and eventually we moved to Murphy Canyon Navy Housing.

When we were notified to move into enlisted quarters, my oldest son Jim was working at the Mataguay Scout Camp. There were no telephones in the camp, and cell phones had not yet made their way into the hands of the general public. So we were unable to tell Jim where or when we were moving. Having the weekend off, Jim went to our rented home in Santee, only to find that we had moved. So he drove up and down the streets of Murphy Canyon (and its 900 houses) until he spotted our car.

He still says that we were trying to get rid of him, but he says that with a big smile on his face.

I was putting things away in the garage while listening to a short wave radio. I was listening to Morse Code in preparation for taking a test, which if passed would earn me a license to operate Ham Radio equipment. Hams were required to receive Morse Code and to take a written test on electronic theory, and national and international law.

The door to the garage was open and the code sounds could be heard out into the street. Enter Bernard J. Rettzo or "BJ." He walked into the garage where I was working and asked why I was listening to CW.[14] When I explained, he said, "Well, I am a Ham and I need you to come over to my house across the street and help me put up a new beam antenna," he remarked.

---

14 CW is Ham-speak for Morse Code.

He didn't mean later or when I could spare the time. He meant at that very moment. Thus started what has turned out to be a life- long friendship!

The antenna was huge even by amateur radio standards, so we worked on the installation for the rest of the day and into the early evening. When I finally did get back to our quarters, my wife was up- set for my having suddenly disappeared, leaving her alone to put away our belongings. Of course, she had no idea where I had gone or what I was doing.

Two weeks later, BJ asked me to accompany him to a local radio store. I didn't question why. After all, it was always fun going to the "candy store." When we got there, BJ pointed to the back room and said, "Now go take your test." I really didn't think that I was ready, but I took the test and passed. Years later, I would return the favor by giving BJ the books needed to complete aviation ground school so that he could earn his private pilot's license.

Chapter 3.9 Intrigue in the Murphy Canyon Little League

My youngest son, Raymond, wasn't into Scouting. He wanted to play Little League baseball. At that time, Murphy Canyon had the nation's largest Little League with about fifty teams. Raymond registered and waited to see which team he would draw. The call came a few nights later. Raymond would not get to play unless I signed up as manager or coach of a newly formed team. I signed up as team manager and went looking for a coach. I looked no farther than across the street. BJ was reluctant because he had about as much organized baseball experience as I did: None. But finally he relented and agreed to be the coach. We went to our first league meeting the next Saturday. The name of our team was the Athletics, or the A's for short.

That weekend, BJ and I went to the ball field to select team members from those kids who still had not been picked up by other teams. Obviously, Ray would be on our team. BJ selected the players he wanted, and we started practicing the following week. Like almost all teams, there were kids with some Little League experience, and some with absolutely no experience playing any kind of organized team sport. It would be a learning experience for everyone.

BJ is one of the most amazing people I ever met. He was a gruff Philadelphia kid who says that he grew up on the wrong side of the tracks. But he has a brain that works on all cylinders. He memorized the rule book in one evening. That memory would come in handy later in the season. BJ proved to be a good coach too. About all I knew how to do was to hit the ball: I had been a pretty good batter when I was a kid.

BJ espoused the philosophy that baseball was basically a game of defense. If you had a flawless defense you would win because sooner or later you would get a run. If you denied the opposing team the chance to score, you win. That became the team philosophy. But first we had to teach the kids how to play the game in accordance with the rules. My philosophy was that the kids should have fun, learn how to play the game, and learn good sportsmanship. I didn't really care how many games we might win, *but the kids sure did.*

The A's were scheduled to play the season opener against the best team in the league. The members of that team had played together for a couple of years, so they had the advantage. Their manager, Joe, was also a Master-at-Arms chief petty officer. I knew him by reputation, but we had never been stationed together. By the end of the season I wished that I had never heard of Joe.

The two teams met on the baseball field one afternoon after school let out. The first thing Joe did was to ask umpires to check to see if our players were wearing the required protective cup as part of their uniform. Most weren't.

The A's were given fifteen minutes to go home and get the required apparel or forfeit the game. Enough of the team got back to the ballpark in time for the game to begin.

The A's suffered a humiliating loss. The kids were embarrassed at being caught without their protective cups and they made basic mistakes that cost them dearly. We emphasized the basics at the next few practices, and BJ kept working on defense. I kept working on batting. However, the A's did have at least one real power hitter who needed no coaching from me.

The A's won the next several games, and as their confidence grew, they began functioning well as a team. BJ kept hammering at the need for a flawless defense and the players could see that it was working. In the first half of the season the A's lost two games which placed them in second place. The winner of the second half of the season would play the winner of the first half for the championship.

The A's won all of their games in the early part of the second half. Joe was not only a team manager, he was also a league official. And in that capacity, he tried to have me removed from the league when I over-pitched our best pitcher by one inning. The league scorekeeper had quit and I had no way of knowing when a pitcher had reached his or her limit. We didn't have a team scorekeeper. League officials decided that I should be suspended for three games. I couldn't even be in the ball park, so I stood on the public street so that the kids on my team could see that I was still there for them.

In the last part of the second half, BJ decided he did not want me telling him how the game should be played, so he quit. BJ was daring, always willing to take chances. I was conservative when we had the lead and wanted to protect our lead by not taking so many chances. The A's lost the next two games. I went to see BJ and we settled on the fact that managers do have the final say, but that the coach's opinion had to be considered. When BJ returned, the A's started winning again. Yes, he was that good, and that important to the players.

A local newspaper writer attended some of the games and wrote a really nice article about how the A's were not getting involved in parental intrigue; how we were just playing good solid baseball. The paper came out on a Friday evening. By Saturday morning, someone had gone around to all of the newspaper vending machines and stolen the newspapers. There was also a rumor that someone had broken into the newspaper office and had stolen the papers there too. That's how nasty the rivalry within the league had become. The atmosphere was so nasty that I stopped attending league meetings.

The A's won the second half, which meant that they would play Joe's team for the championship. The two teams met on a Saturday afternoon. It was one of those flawless San Diego Chamber of Commerce afternoons—warm but not hot. With blue skies and a few puffy white clouds, it was a perfect day for baseball.

Two days before the championship game, we lost our heavy hitter. A team from the next higher division drafted our best player. I was frustrated because the higher division team had finished for the season and would not play again that year. I complained to league officials that since the higher division had no more games to play, they should not have the right to draft our best player, thereby depriving him of the privilege of playing in the championship game. I lost the argument.

At that time, the rules clearly gave the senior team the right to draft anyone from a junior team. No timeline was specified. When we got to the ballpark, I had to tell the drafted player that he was no longer a member of the A's. Furthermore, he couldn't even wear the A's uniform. The drafted player peeled off his uniform and sat in the bleachers in his underwear. The league finally let him put on his uniform trousers.

Evidently there was no rule against sitting in the bleachers in underwear, so they couldn't throw him out of the park. But they tried.

I recognized the game's head umpire as being Joe's close friend and fellow league official. He was also a man who had earlier been removed from umpiring any game in which the A's were playing because of his use of foul language and his display of a nasty temper toward the A's team members.

So intense was the parental competition within the Murphy Canyon league that Little League of California sent two representatives from Sacramento to monitor the final game. When I showed them the letter barring the head umpire from officiating at A's games, they ruled that the Murphy Canyon Little League would have to provide another umpire. He was replaced by a man who had an impeccable record for professionalism. At least the game would be officiated fairly and impartially.

I walked to home plate and gave the lineup to the umpires. Joe did the same for his team. I asked the umpires for a decision regarding benching. Three of our poorest players had been benched for three games for attitude infractions, but they had only sat out the previous two games.

"Does the championship game count as game three, or do the benched players have to play?" I asked.

The officials discussed the question and decided that the players should remain benched during the championship game. I returned to the A's dugout.

Joe asked the umpires to check the A's to see if they were wearing their protective cups. This time, they all had the required gear, and grinned as they thumped their cups as proof for the umpires. Even the girls on the team had worn protective cups, although they didn't have to.

People in the park sang the "Star Spangled Banner." Joe's bleachers were overflowing. His team sponsor, which was the ship he was assigned to, had filled the bleachers with the ship's crew, including the commanding officer.

Our A's had about six parents in the bleachers, and we didn't have a sponsor. It was a really "Bad News Bears" situation.

The first half of the game was fairly even. Joe's team would get a run; the A's would get a run. The score was tied. I started substituting players in the third inning so that we would have our best players on the field in the last innings. Joe didn't start substitutions until the fifth inning. At that level of Little League, only seven innings are played, unless the game was tied and went into overtime.

As the game entered the seventh inning, Joe's players were at bat. The A's pitcher went into his wind-up and threw the ball. The batter hit a double. BJ, without the use of notes or scorekeeping records, told me that the batter was not eligible to be at bat because he had not been out of the game for the specified amount of time.

"Time," I yelled.

The umpire stopped the game. I walked over to home plate where I told the umpire that the batter had not been out of play for the minimum amount of time. He had been brought back in the game too early. The head umpire checked with the league scorekeeper who agreed. "You're out," yelled the umpire pointing to the runner on second base. Joe threw his hat on the ground, yelled a few expletives, and walked back to the dugout where he sent the next batter to the plate.

The A's pitcher wound up, threw the ball, and again, the batter got a double. Again BJ told me that the batter was ineligible.

"Time," I yelled.

I explained that the second batter had also been returned to the lineup too early. And once again the umpire checked with the league scorekeeper and then yelled, "You're out."

As the batter returned to the dugout, Joe began yelling. Then Joe became physical, pushing the boy to the ground.

Early in the seventh inning, our bleachers had filled with parents. On the other side, the bleachers suddenly emptied as the commanding officer and ship's crew abruptly left the ballpark.

The third batter on Joe's team got a hit; the ball went deep into right field. The A's right fielder trapped the ball and made a remarkable throw from right field to home plate. It was the reason why BJ had placed him in right field to begin with. The right fielder's throwing arm was cannon, and it resulted in the game-winning out. As BJ always said, "perfect defense wins games."

The A's players got the hits they needed to win. And they were the league champs for their age group! As they walked off the field, the kids reminded me that my wife had promised at the beginning of the season, that if they won the championship, I would buy all the pizza and soft drinks they could eat and drink. They jumped in the back of my pickup truck eagerly awaiting the trip to the local pizza parlor. They were loud and they were boisterous, as kids will be when celebrating such a momentous moment.

As the designated home team manager, it fell to me to put away the field equipment and to ensure that everything was accounted for. It took about twenty minutes to secure those items that needed to be secured. When I finished, I walked toward my truck and noticed that Joe was talking to the A's ball players who were in the back of my pickup truck. When he saw me approaching, he took off running for his own vehicle. I thought he had been congratulating the boys. Quite the opposite! He was telling them that were not the champions, that they were nothing but a bunch of bums. I assured the kids that they were the champions and that Joe was a poor sport and a sore loser.

The mood quickly passed at the pizza parlor where mass quantities of pizza and soft drinks were consumed. Some of the parents even joined in the revelry.

The kids were champions in every aspect of the word. Although they wanted to, they never gave in to the name calling and intrigue that the other teams did, not even at school. It was one heck of a season. BJ had created in a winning team. That was Saturday.

On Sunday, I stopped by Joe's quarters in naval housing to find out when the final league meeting would take place. The house was empty; no furniture, nothing. Later the next week, I learned that the commanding officer of the ship that had sponsored Joe's team had transferred Joe to another command in Long Beach, all within twenty four hours. His behavior on the field had embarrassed the CO, the ship, and its crew. I never saw or heard of Joe again.

Chapter 3.10 New Job at the Naval Station

(January 1980)

During the year and a half that I was assigned to eradicating drugs and reducing vandalism at the barracks, the naval station won first and second place in competition for the Zumwalt Award for best barracks on a large installation. The drug dealers had taken their cash and had moved to the city, and the vandalism went from a hundred thousand dollars a year to just ten dollars. During that time, I attended various drug and narcotics classes with the U. S. Drug Enforcement Administration, and advanced explosives investigations school with the U.S. Bureau of Alcohol, Tobacco, and Firearms (ATF).

The barracks cleanup was so successful that the naval station commanding officer decided to expand the investigation of drugs and narcotics to the rest of the base. I was moved to the police building, Investigations Division, where with two other military police investigators we bagged thirty drug dealers in thirty days.

My favorite busts were the pizza delivery guy who was delivering pizza and drugs to personnel on ships that were tied up to piers on the naval station, and the newspaper delivery man, who was similarly delivering drugs with his newspapers.

It was about that time that the civilian Chief of Police decided to leave the department. Senior Chief Durazo had already rotated to his next command. One Monday morning, a civilian police captain told me to report to the Security Officer; a lieutenant commander who was the military department head for the Security Department.

Working drugs and narcotics meant that I normally wore civilian clothes. I kept no uniform at the office. I went to the boss's office and was immediately ushered in. The Security Officer said, "You're the new Chief of Police. Get into uniform and get to work." I said that I would need something in writing, especially for the civilian employees. The security officer scrawled out a hand printed note designating me as the acting chief of police. So in the blink of an eye, I went from investigator to the Chief of Police of a large military law enforcement and security organization.

Although the appointment was only to be an interim measure until a new civilian chief was hired, the base CO decided that I would remain as the police chief for the remainder of my time at the naval station, about another year and a half.

Chapter 3.11 New Police Strategies

(January 1980)

The Naval Station Police Department was comprised of military and civilian police officers and civilian guards who staffed guard posts on the base, and at recreation areas including the Murphy Canyon Golf Course, which belonged to the naval station. Military and civilian personnel barely got along with each other. The guards, most of who were in their late fifties and early sixties, didn't get along very well with the police officers, military or civilian. Few, if any, of the military personnel were rated Master-at-Arms.

Little attention had been paid to the plight of the guards, who had really boring jobs. Consequently, they didn't do the jobs very well. If a car had a decal and the driver had a military or civilian identification card, the guards would let them in. They never really looked at the car or the people inside the vehicle to determine whether they represented a threat to the base or its personnel. It was a nowhere job, and that's the way they liked it.

I visited all of the guard posts during the midnight watch. The guards were shocked to see the Chief of Police. I was told that no police chief had ever visited guards on the mid-watch before. There were no heaters in the guard shacks. San Diego does get cold, especially between midnight and dawn in the winter months.

The comptroller denied my request for money to buy space heaters, so I went to the commanding officer and requested the money as a matter of personnel safety rather than for comfort. The CO ordered the comptroller to find the money.

Some of the guards had been standing post for ten or fifteen years. No one had ever paid attention to their needs, so they were both surprised and grateful when the heaters were installed. Now that they were more comfortable, I had to find ways to keep them awake while they were on duty.

I visited the guards at odd hours. I warned, and then fired a couple of security guards for sleeping. The rest of the guards got the message. I also ordered the shift supervisors (civilian police captains) to visit every guard post at least once during their shift. That order made the captains unhappy because they usually sat on their butts at headquarters.

Murphy Canyon Navy Housing is situated on a bluff high above the Navy golf course. I received a report one night at about midnight that a guard at the golf course was calling for a shotgun to be delivered to his post. Why, I asked?

"Dunno," was the answer.

I jumped into my private vehicle (even as the Chief of Police, I wasn't allowed to drive the police car to my quarters) and went to the guard post. The shotgun had already been delivered. There on the raised island of the guard post was the largest, fattest rattlesnake that I had ever seen. Rattlesnakes at the golf course fed on the hundreds of rabbits that fed on the grass at night. The snakes grew large on the easy prey. I ordered that a shotgun be issued daily to guards at the golf course. Evidently, over the years, the guards had several rattlesnake stories, but everyone thought that they were exaggerating. They weren't.

The law enforcement side of the department was reactive rather than proactive. I required the officers to attend preliminary investigations and crime prevention classes. I forced the police officers to use the tools they had been given in class. Every police officer was an investigator. They looked at cases with new eyes. They started solving crimes. Each police officer was also a crime prevention specialist. They would walk the barracks area when they weren't responding to a call. They met and talked with the residents. They made recommendations as to how theft and other crimes could be prevented around the barracks. In the first year that I was chief of police, crime was reduced on the naval station by over forty percent. I'm still proud of that record.

Chapter 3.12 Planning My Next Duty Assignment

Within six months of my planned rotation date, the date that I would leave for my next assignment, the detailer told me that I would be assigned to the *USS Vancouver* (LPD-2). I would have to catch up with the ship in Australia. I was really looking forward to seeing Australia. But once again, it was not to be.

I was surprised when I got a call from the Commanding Officer of the *USS Vancouver* or "Vancan" as it was called by the crew. The CO wanted me to terminate shore duty early and to deploy with the ship. I explained that my daughter was to be married in a few months, and that I didn't want to be stuck on a ship overseas. The CO said that he would guarantee leave so that I could attend the wedding. But, since it would cost about three thousand dollars for roundtrip airfare, I declined. There wasn't anything the ship's CO could do, but he tried. He called the Chief of Naval Operations citing "needs of his ship." However the commanding officer at the naval station said the naval station's needs were just as necessary. I was allowed to stay in San Diego while the ship deployed.

Chapter 3.13 Applying for LDO

Along with all of the other paperwork that came across my desk, was an announcement that the Navy was going to select the first limited duty physical security officers and warrant officers. I had dreamed of being the Navy's first designated security officer since the beginning of the Master-at-Arms program. In fact, I had been severely criticized by peers and senior petty officers for espousing that ambition over the years.

I worked on my officer selection package for weeks and finally submitted it with great trepidation. I was junior to many of the Master-at-Arms personnel who would also submit packages for consideration. I was convinced that politics would be the deciding factor. I was never politically correct. I was, however, very respectful of others, especially my seniors. Over the years, I had crossed swords with a lot of people, especially with those NIS Agents who were content to sit on their butts instead of getting out and doing the leg work required of investigations. I was convinced that I would not be selected, but I remained hopeful.

With the wedding over and the rotation date arrived, it was time for me to move on to my new duty assignment on the USS Vancouver (LPD-2).

CHAPTER FOUR

Chapter 4.1 Temporary Additional Duty (TAD) in Hawaii

I was standing in line to get airline tickets for the flight to Australia where I was to meet the USS Vancouver, when one of the clerks shouted, "Is there was a Chief Cline in the office?" I answered up, and the clerk handed me the phone saying that it was the naval station CO. When I answered the phone, the captain said, "Hey John, where do you think you're going?"

I answered, "Australia."

The CO laughed and said, "No you're not, you're getting tickets to Hawaii. You have new orders."

I went to the captain's office and picked up the new orders; what the Navy calls TAD or Temporary Additional Duty orders. I was being diverted to an admiral's staff in Hawaii where I was to conduct an investigation. Upon completion of the investigation, and when released by the admiral, I would resume my trip to the Vancan. I had no idea why I had been selected, or what kind of investigation that I was to conduct. I got tickets to Hawaii and a couple of days later, after saying goodbye to my family, flew to Hawaii.

I proceeded directly to the admiral's office. The admiral wasn't available, but the secretary indicated that the admiral wanted me to meet him for dinner at the Officer's Club. I checked into the Chief's Barracks and shifted to civilian clothes and went to the O'Club to meet the admiral at the appointed hour. During dinner, the admiral said that he suspected one of his shipboard commanding officers of using narcotics or other drugs. I was to conduct a discreet investigation to prove or disprove the allegations.

The investigation took the better part of a week. The offending captain was forced to retire after admitting that he was addicted to heroin, which was consistent with the findings of my investigation.

The admiral was delighted with my very quiet and low-profile investigation.

As the admiral and I discussed the details of the case, he said, "Oh by the way, you were selected for the LDO program, Ensign." I couldn't believe what he had said. The admiral laughed and showed me the selection list. The selection board had selected two Limited Duty Officers (LDOs) and three Warrant Officers for the Navy's security program. The other LDO was a female Master-at Arms who had been my classmate in MA School. Like me, she had been junior to many of the other Master-at-Arms.

The MA detailer confirmed that I had been selected for the LDO program. In the past, chief petty officers who were selected for the LDO program started their officer careers as a lieutenant junior grade (LTJG), not ensign. The Navy, however, had decided to change the rules so that they conformed to other services. However, that change wasn't scheduled to begin for another year. The detailer said that the Secretary of the Navy had decided to start early and "if you don't like it, don't accept the commission." Yeah, right! I called my wife, Pat, to tell her the good news. Her response was, "You mean we will have a blue sticker (on the car)?

"Yes, we will get a blue sticker." That also meant that we would have to move from enlisted housing to officer housing.

The Admiral invited me to remain on his staff until the ship returned to Hawaii from the western Pacific. However, he also informed me that the *Vancouver's* Commanding Officer had been "burning up the airwaves" to the Chief of Naval Operations about my unscheduled TAD orders to Hawaii. Once again, of course, the Vancan CO lost the argument, since it had been the Chief of Naval Personnel who had recommended me for the job in Hawaii. I was told that the Vancan CO was fuming mad.

As much as I would have liked to stay in Hawaii, I felt that duty required that I report to the ship. I thanked the admiral for the offer, got airline tickets to the Philippines, and then flew to Manila where I caught up with the *USS Vancouver* at Subic Bay.

Official U.S. Navy photo
USS Vancouver (LPD-2)

Chapter 4.2 USS Vancouver (LPD-2)

I checked into the Chief's Barracks at Naval Station Subic Bay and went to the CPO club for dinner. The ship came in the following morning. I checked on board and went to the chief's locker, sometimes called the goat locker (as in old goats) where I was told that the captain had been extremely angry over my delay and that I would likely suffer great torments. The chiefs were looking forward to seeing how the CO was going to torture the new sheriff for not leaving San Diego with the ship, and for going TAD to Hawaii. I wasn't looking forward to the confrontation one little bit.

The next morning, I met with the ship's executive officer. He too said that he was expecting the captain to have my head. Great! Then I unloaded the next bit of news. I would only be on the ship for about six months because I had been selected for the LDO program. The XO just rolled his eyes. (Executive officers must learn how to roll their eyes at XO School). The XO really didn't want to have to tell the captain, so he didn't.

I had been on the ship for nearly two weeks and still I had not met the captain. I was standing in the passageway outside of the XO's quarters for "Officer's Call," where department heads and the Chief Master-at-Arms report to the Executive Officer with evening reports. The captain stuck his head into the XO's office to give him some last minute instructions. As the CO resumed walking through the passageway, he noticed me standing in line with the officers. The XO, who by then was following the captain, rolled his eyes again.

"When did you get aboard?" the Captain asked. "I met the ship in Subic Bay," I said.

"How long have you been aboard?" "A little over a week, sir."

The captain turned to the XO and said, "Bring the chief to my cabin when you're through with Officer's Call."

"Yes sir," said a very pale XO.

SEA STORIES AND NAVY TALES

Officer's Call didn't last long that night. Everyone expected that I would be dismembered, keelhauled, or at the very least, receive some form of verbal torture at the hands of the captain because of his pent up frustrations.

The XO led the way to captain's cabin. He knocked on the door and when authorized, stepped into the cabin. I followed. The XO introduced me and told the captain that I had been selected for LDO and would only be on the ship a few months. The captain looked angrily at the XO and said, "Shut the door on your way out."

The XO had been dismissed. I thought that I saw a bit of relief on his face. I braced for the coming onslaught.

The captain reached over and shook my hand, saying how glad he was that I was finally on board the ship. He poured coffee and told me how angry he had been when he first got the news that I had been diverted. He asked how the wedding went. In short, he was a perfect host and gentleman. He never once uttered an angry word.

He asked what I thought of the ship. I told him that it was clean and that crew's morale seemed to be good. The CO beamed. Then I told him that the crew had been leaning on the lifelines when the ship came into port. They should have been standing at attention. A flash of anger crossed the CO's eyes, and then he said, "I expect you to correct that situation when we pass the Arizona." I assured him that the crew would stand tall upon entering port and passing the Arizona Memorial. We talked about the Captain's expectations. Then the CO said again how good it was that I was aboard. I was dismissed.

When I returned to the chief's mess, every chief who was not on watch was waiting with great anticipation. They even stopped the movie to hear how the captain had dismembered me. They wanted to see the blood. They wanted to hear the anguish in my voice as I explained how the captain had verbally ground me up like raw meat. They were really disappointed when I told them how nice the he had been. For them, it was very anticlimactic.

The ship headed for the Gulf of Oman on a secret mission. We had a full load of Marines, and the Marines were bored. There wasn't a lot for Marines to do on the ship when we were at sea, so a few of them tended to get into trouble from time to time.

Chapter 4.3 Getting to Know the Crew

(October 1980)

One Marine in particular was hell bent on trouble. He was a large Samoan who had just gotten out of the brig at Subic Bay where he had spent several months for having attacked and seriously hurt several Shore Patrolmen. He was creating a disturbance on the mess decks when I first confronted him. The Marine said that he wasn't afraid of me or my rank, and indicated that he had already seriously hurt several other "cops," and that "an old man like me would be no problem." Old man? I was only forty-one.

I grabbed him by the ear and said in a whisper, "Listen up, I believe you would hurt me. And because I do believe you, the law allows me to shoot you dead if you attack me. All I have to do is prove that you threatened me, and I have plenty of witnesses to prove that." The Marine went below deck without further conversation.

There was a real potential for violence between the Marines and sailors during the months to come. Marines and sailors love to hate each other until someone outside of the fraternity steps in. Then Marines and sailors fight for each other. So I went to the Executive Officer asking for some Marines to be assigned to the Master-at-Arms force. The XO referred me to the CO of the embarked Marines, a colonel.

The colonel said he would put out the word and that I could interview volunteers in the morning. True to his word, ten Marines stood outside the MA office to be interviewed. The first Marine in line was the very large Samoan that I had tangled with the evening before.

I explained the types of duties that would be required. Then I asked the Samoan Marine why he wanted to work as a Master-at- Arms.

He said, "No one ever stood up to me before."

He was one of the six Marines who were chosen for MA duties. Having Marines on the master-at-arms force proved to be a good idea. There were absolutely no problems with sailors or Marines during the entire cruise.

Chapter 4.4 Attempted Rescue of American Hostages

There were several chiefs on the ship with whom I grew especially fond. The chief who I liked best was known as "Muck." He was a Navy SEAL who was in charge of the SEAL Team that was embarked on the ship for a secret mission. He and his team were to go into Iran and participate in the rescue of the U.S. Embassy personnel who were being held hostage by Iranian students and the Iranian Guard. When aircraft assigned to the rescue mechanically failed, the mission was tragically called off.

Eventually the ship headed back to San Diego, with stops in Guam and Hawaii. We refueled in Guam and headed out that same day. After another week at sea, we approached Hawaii. The Marines would dis-embark and Tigers would ride the Vancan back to San Diego. While passing the Arizona Memorial, the ship's crew and the Marines stood at attention and saluted. No one was leaning on the lifelines. They looked really smart!

The ship tied up to its assigned berth. It took longer than usual to clear customs. Only when we did finally clear both customs and the health service could personnel be allowed on and off of the ship. As the Marines were leaving the ship, the Samoan approached me and asked me to step off the ship to meet his rather extensive family, all of whom were standing on the pier. I felt honored that the Marine would want me to meet them. Over the next few years, I have often wondered how the Samoan's life turned out.

Chapter 4.5 Who Are You, Really?

I was called to the CO's cabin. "Have a seat." The captain looked hard into my eyes and asked, "Who are you really?"

"Sir?" I asked, clearly confused by the question?

"Come on," the captain continued. "That Navy band out there on the pier is for you, not for the ship. Also, the admiral sent orders that I was to personally hand you his car keys and ask you to meet him for lunch tomorrow at the Officer's Club. The admiral also invited you stay at his home on the north side of the island. Who are you really? No chief petty officer gets that kind of treatment from an admiral," he said.

I just smiled.

Then the captain in a subdued voice asked, "Could you drop me off at the O'Club? I don't have a car." After dropping off the Captain, I had to hurry to pick up my youngest son, Raymond, who had flown to Hawaii for the Tiger Cruise.

The ship was to leave the following day, so there would only be one evening to see a little of Hawaii. I elected not stay at the admiral's house as I don't feel comfortable staying in the homes of friends and acquaintances. Because I had Raymond with me, I didn't think it was appropriate. Ray and I spent the evening in Honolulu.

As we walked along Hotel Street, we were accosted by a half dozen hookers. Raymond was big for his age, but still he looked young. The prostitutes started grabbing at him, asking if he had ever had sex with a woman. He blushed and I told them to get lost. We kept walking. Raymond, a teenager, was proud of the fact that he had been accosted by hookers. Later, his mother was horrified when she heard the story. We went to the Hale Koa Hotel on the beach at Waikiki, an Armed Forces Recreation Center for military personnel that provides lodging, dinning, and entertainment. I thought that it would less expensive than the other hotels. But it sure wasn't cheap!

After dinner, we walked around, visiting several of Waikiki's hotels and poking our noses into many of the shops along Ala Moana Boulevard. Then we headed back to the ship for a night's sleep before we set sail the next day.

Late the next morning, I shifted to civilian clothes to join the admiral for lunch at the O'Club. Ray stayed on the ship. As I was being seated at the admiral's table, I saw the ship's captain in the buffet line. I asked the admiral if he would mind if the CO joined us. The admiral approved my request, and I invited the captain to meet the admiral and to have lunch with us. The captain didn't want to, but finally relented at my repeated urging. It was only during lunch that I learned what had happened when the ship had pulled into port. Seated at the table with the admiral, the captain was noticeably uneasy.

It turned out that the admiral and his chief of staff had met the ship when we arrived. The executive officer would not allow them to board because the ship had not yet cleared customs. The admiral became angry at being rebuffed, so he and the chief of staff returned to their offices. Later, after cancelling the CO's car and some other perks that ship's captains normally get, the chief of staff returned to the ship and gave the CO the keys to the admiral's car with specific instructions as to what he was to tell the *Vancouver's* Chief Master-at-Arms.

The captain remained uneasy throughout lunch, and asked to be excused soon after finishing his hurriedly eaten meal. The admiral and I continued talking until he too had to return to his office. I made my way back to the ship, after having returned the Admiral's car, and got ready to set sail early that evening.

Raymond was sick for the first three days at sea, missing all of the planned activities for Tigers. He also woke up all the chiefs at about 0200 the first night by yelling a blood-curdling scream in his sleep. He scared the hell out of everyone in the chief's quarters, especially me.

With no Marines on the ship, most of the spaces below the main deck were empty. Keeping the spaces clean meant that sailors would have the added chore of cleaning those spaces in addition to their own. It also meant that there were plenty of places to hide and use drugs. Since I no longer had Marines on the MA force, patrolling the ship was accomplished by six temporary MA's.

Like the *USS Chicago*, each department had activities for the Tigers, but because the Vancan didn't have the weapons of a cruiser, there wasn't very much for the Tigers to do. So they watched a lot of movies. Those who were seasick slept a lot.

A few weeks after the ship's arrival in San Diego, the CO made the transition to his next duty station and a new captain took command. He arrived just in time to put the ship in dry-dock for extensive repairs. I had been selected for promotion to senior chief. The new captain indicated that since I was going to be an Ensign in a few weeks, he saw no reason to promote me to senior chief. However, the official record would reflect that I was a permanent grade senior chief even after I entered the LDO program. LDOs retain their enlisted status until they make Lieutenant Commander, at which time they have to declare whether they will revert back to their enlisted grade or accept a permanent commission as a Lieutenant Commander.

Chapter 4.6 The Four Star Hotel

The USS Vancouver went into a shipyard for major repairs and upgrades. Even the enlisted living quarters required modification, so the crew was to live on barges. Life on barges means that you have no space of your own. A bunk used at night by a day shift person is then used during the day by a night shift person. There were no lockers to secure personal possessions. It's just a lousy way to have to live for months at a time.

Since San Diego was our home port, most of the married men lived ashore. But there were a significant number of personnel who lived on the ship. I went to the San Diego Hotel that was itself being renovated. There were about a 150 rooms that were still being used, but most people who stay in four-star hotels would rather go to a hotel that wasn't being remodeled. Rooms at the San Diego Hotel, for the most part, sat empty. After talking with the manager, arrangements were made for the crew to reside at the hotel at a greatly reduced price. I reported to the captain and suggested that use of the hotel would be better than living on barges, which came at a cost too. The captain agreed, and the crew moved to the hotel.

Although there were two men to a room, the crew loved it. They got to stay in a four-star hotel for the entire time that enlisted berthing underwent repairs and modifications. Living in the hotel was my parting gift to the crew.

Chapter 4.7 Transitioning to the Officer Corps

The day finally came on April 1, 1981, when I was discharged from the Navy as a Senior Chief Petty Officer and commissioned as a Limited Duty Officer, Ensign. I didn't realize just then how difficult the transition from chief to ensign would be. As a chief, I had the rest of the chief's community to consult with when I needed help or encouragement. The officer community was not so close, especially if you were a physical security officer.

I called my former commanding officer from the *USS Chicago,* who had recently retired. I wanted to share the news of my good fortune. When the retired captain heard the news, he said, "Now that you are a commissioned officer, don't ever call me again." After which, he abruptly hung up. I was stunned.

I called another former commanding officer, a captain in the Naval Reserve. The captain said that I had made a huge mistake; that although I had been a good chief, I would never make it in the "officer world."

As an enlisted man, I had pretty much lived up to the world's expectations of being an enlisted man. As a commissioned officer, I held myself to a much higher standard, but still managed to have some fun and to get myself into trouble.

Pat and I hosted a "wetting down" party for our friends, mainly the chiefs from the *USS Vancouver.* The term "wetting down" refers to wetting the new officer bars with saltwater so that they won't look so shiny. Shiny ensign's bars are a sure sign of a newly commissioned officer. However, we wet down the new shiny bars, and each other, with beer and booze rather than with saltwater. Following the wetting down, it was time to move on to new adventures.

CHAPTER FIVE

Chapter 5.1 Another New Beginning

I was a 42 year old ensign; probably the oldest ensign in the Navy at the time, and possibly the oldest peacetime ensign in naval history. I would have been a lieutenant junior grade (LTJG) but for the decision of the Secretary of the Navy who had decided that chiefs entering the LDO program should start at ensign, like other services. He implemented that policy a year earlier than required, catching me and others in the wake of his decision. Yes, I resented his decision.

My wife and I were still in bed when the detailer called. It was two hours later in Washington D.C. than it was in San Diego. The detailer wanted to know where I wanted to go for my first assignment as an officer. His preference was for me to go to Naval Station Roosevelt Roads in Puerto Rico, but he would allow me to fill a billet in Spain. The detailer didn't want to assign me to the one and only security billet in Washington D.C., because he wanted to fill that position with the new female LDO. So, I did what any good brand new naval officer would do: I asked my wife where she wanted to go. There was a lot to say for going to Europe, but Pat chose Puerto Rico because it wasn't quite as far away from San Diego. I asked the detailer why he thought Puerto Rico would be the better assignment.

"That's where the action is," he said.

Chapter 5.2 Terrorism in Puerto Rico

Terrorism in Puerto Rico has mainly been about a minority of people who want independence. The majority of people in Puerto Rico have voted (at least twice) not to seek independence.

There were two principal groups that advocated the use of violence to achieve independence: The Ejército Popular Boricua (Boricua Popular/Peoples Army) and the Los Macheteros, known locally as the Machete Wielders or the Cane Cutters. They were also known as the Puerto Rican Popular Army.

Puerto Rican nationalists have been attacking Americans for years. Probably the first notable incidents were the attacks on the residence of President Truman in 1950, followed by the gun-blazing attack on the U.S. House of Representatives in 1954. Four Puerto Rican separatists unfurled a Puerto Rican flag and began shooting automatic pistols from the Ladies Gallery at the representatives on the floor of the House who were debating an immigration bill.[15]

Following their arrest and trials, President Eisenhower commuted their death sentences to a minimum of 70 years in prison. After 25 years, President Jimmy Carter granted pardons as a "humanitarian" gesture."[16]

However, it also may have been part of a deal cut with Fidel Castro, who "as a humanitarian gesture" simultaneously released several American CIA agents who were being held in Cuba on espionage charges. President Carter steadfastly denied that a deal had been made.

---

15 Source: Wikipedia – last checked on 4/1/2008 at http://en.wikipedia. org/wiki/U.S._Capitol_shooting_incident_(1954)

16 Ibid

Three attacks by the Macheteros had obviously been on the minds of Navy brass when they created the physical security officer billet in Puerto Rico. The more recent attack occurred in January of 1981. Members of the Los Macheteros entered Muniz Air National Guard Base where they destroyed or damaged ten Air Force A-7 Corsairs and a F-104 fighter jet. They caused about $45 million dollars in damages. The attackers were not identified, and no arrests had been made.

Two earlier attacks by the Macheteros were probably of more importance to the Navy. In December 1979, members of the Macheteros shot up a Navy bus transporting sailors to work at the Sabana Seca Naval Communications Station near San Juan. Two Navy personnel were killed and ten sailors were wounded. Also in 1979, an attack by the Macheteros killed one sailor and wounded three others in retaliation for the murder of a Macheteros member who was in prison. Allegedly, he had been killed by prison guards, who the Macheteros perceived to be retired Marines.

I didn't tell Pat about the potential for terrorism.

Chapter 5.3 Returning to Lackland Air Force Base

(May 1981)

No "Sailors Have More Fun" stickers this time. Two Navy warrant officers and I went to the Air Force law enforcement for commissioned officers' class. We were the first naval officers ever to attend that course. The rest of the class, consisting of about twenty students, was made up of Air Force officers who were also being assigned to law enforcement and security functions. There's not a lot of difference between Navy warrant officers and limited duty officers. We both do the same job. However, warrant officers, although junior to commissioned officers, do have a certain distinction that ensigns don't have.

The officer's security course dealt primarily with security during missile movement, weapons facilities, and flightline security, things that were most important to Air Force security. There was almost nothing mentioned about law enforcement. Since the naval officers didn't anticipate becoming involved with missile movement, I asked the instructors if we could play the role of the bad guys. The instructors agreed. Each day, the instructors threw different scenarios at the students.

Repelling an attack during missile movement proved to be both an art and a science. Each student officer had to play the role of an Air Force security person, starting at the rear wheel of the last vehicle, working his way up through each position in the convoy until they had experienced the role of every security component, including Convoy Commander. Because there were about twenty five people in the class, there were a lot of problems for class members to overcome.

Students donned special tactical gear that would determine whether a shot was a hit resulting in a disabling wound, a kill, or a miss. We drew weapons and spent most of our days in the field. Getting out of the classroom and into the field was fun, especially for us bad guys. After we had a look at the terrain, we would lay in wait for the convoy and attack using strategies that we collectively devised earlier in the day. The bad guys always won. Never once did the class out maneuver the naval officers or overcome our tactics. Not a good thing if you are supposed to be protecting a missile convoy from falling into terrorist hands. It was determined that the three naval officers made good terrorists. Too good, in fact!

The class was assigned to protect a flightline with fighter jets. We, the naval officers were the terrorists, of course. Crawling on our bellies, we easily overcame student guards and used their security radios to taunt the rest of the student security personnel who were assigned to either apprehend us, or to kill us in the event we failed to surrender.

As a squad of student security police made their way toward us, the two Navy warrant officers outflanked the squad and took their commander (a female second lieutenant who had never before been faced with ground tactics) hostage. The naval officer- terrorists moved their hostage under the wing of one of the aircraft on the flight line. I asked the hostage to speak into the radio so that the rest of the class would know that we had captured their commander. She refused.

I grabbed a handful of her hair and yanked--hard. She yelled out in pain. The radio was keyed so that the good guys could hear her yell. Then in broken Spanish, I proclaimed that we were the Los Macheteros, and if the second squad of student security police that was making its way toward us didn't back off, the hostage would be killed, and we would blow up the aircraft. For a while, it was a standoff.

It should be noted herein that in the normal course of training, students always removed the antennas from their handheld radios so that only those who were actually involved in the class could hear the radio transmissions. That was good in theory, but it failed in practice.

The Lackland Air Force Base Security Police were alerted to the "terrorist incident" and they came loaded for bear with live ammunition. Luckily for the class, someone had the good sense to realize that this just might be a training situation and although ready for the real thing, approached the instructors to determine the status of the incident.

The commander of the base police said the transmissions were so real that they had set off alerts throughout the base. The commanding general had a few choice words for the instructors, who then had a few choice words for me. We lost our position as the class bad guys and were returned to regular status as student good guys. But that didn't work to the advantage of the instructors either. When we were the bad guys, we were really bad. When we were the good guys, we were really good.

In another scenario, the class was placed in a simulated weapons storage area. Our job was to keep the weapons secure from known terrorists who were going to try to take over the depot to steal nuclear weapons. I was the officer in command.

What made the scenario different was that enlisted personnel who were simultaneously attending security classes for weapons depot security would be playing the functions that they would actually perform when they got out into the real world.

The officers filled supervisory positions. This was the first time that student enlisted personnel participated with officers in the field. They didn't know the officers, and the officers didn't know them. It proved to be a challenge.

Officer and enlisted personnel were placed throughout the weapons depot in accordance with Air Force security policy. The terrorists (our instructors) attacked. During the firefight, I noticed two airmen lying on top of a bunker trying to get off some shots at the "terrorists." Now that may look good in the movies, but lying on top of a bunker only a few feet higher than the rest of the ground presents a beautiful silhouette target for the bad guys. I came up behind the two airmen and grabbed them by the seat of their pants and dragged them down the side of the bunker. I scared the hell out of them because they didn't know anyone was behind them, and they certainly never expected anyone to grab them by the seat of their pants. But then I was embarrassed when I realized that both of the airmen I had grabbed were young women. I explained that they were making a target of themselves by lying on top of the bunker. I then demonstrated a better way to shoot, using the side of the bunker to provide some degree of protection.

Somehow, the instructor-terrorists were able to successfully take over the guard tower in the center of the depot. The guard in the tower should have been able to see the unauthorized personnel well before they got inside the compound. With rifles being fired throughout the compound, the depot was in pandemonium. Finally, the instructors came out on the ledge of the tower with their hostage and threatened to kill him if the students did not throw down their weapons and lay face down on the ground in a field in front of the tower.

I got on the radio (everyone had a handheld radio) and told the officers and enlisted personnel to do as they were told. There was a lot of grumbling about my order, but as I was the officer in command, they did as they were told.

The instructor-terrorists had made a tactical error, and I wanted to take advantage of their mistake. All of the instructors were in the tower. Even with the advantage of height, they couldn't watch forty or more people at the same time. The Navy warrant officers and I remained well out of view of the instructors who were on the ledge of the guard tower. We naval officers each took two fully loaded M-16s and a dozen hand grenades, and made our way underneath the guard tower where we were not visible to the instructor-terrorists above. Eventually, the instructor-terrorists handcuffed the guard inside the tower and returned to the ledge to supervise the total surrender of the student security force. That's when we opened fire.

The attack scared the instructors because they weren't expecting to be shot at since they believed everyone had surrendered. They never saw us. They had to admit that they were, for all practical purposes, dead. By staying together, exposed on the ledge, they had made a tactical error that cost them the scenario.

After killing the terrorists, I redeployed the security force throughout the compound in accordance with Air Force policy, and the exercise ended. The good guys had won again.

Chapter 5.4 The Lackland Admiral

(May 1981)

Not everything in the security officer's class at Lackland was work-related. Fridays on the base included an evening happy hour at the Officer's Club. Unlike Navy clubs, which are free, Army and Air Force clubs charged a fairly hefty annual fee for being a "member." You couldn't enter the club unless you were a member. So, grumbling, we three naval officers paid the fee and went to the O'Club for Happy Hour on Fridays. At least the drinks and meals were a little less expensive than they were in town.

Lackland Air Force Base was primarily a training facility. Not only was it the training facility for the Air Force Security Police, it was also the enlisted "boot camp." Another command that was attached to the base was the Wilford Hall Medical Center, which along with its other medical missions, was a training hospital for new medical personnel, including nurses.

The nurses, being newly commissioned officers, also made their way to happy hour at the O'Club on Fridays. Flight crews from Kelly Air Force Base related stories of daring-do to the delight of the newly commissioned nurses. On any given Friday, you could find a group of Air Force nurses seated in the bar surrounded by a group of pilots. That would soon change.

The class of Security Officers also went to the O'Club for Happy Hour. We were required to wear dress uniforms on Fridays, which was graduation day for recruits. For naval officers, wearing a dress uniform meant wearing summer whites.

A Navy cover (hat) placed on the hat rack in the lobby of the O'Club was an automatic invitation for any Air Force Officer to steal it as a trophy for having "put one over on the Navy." Since there was no Navy Exchange in the area, the luckless naval officer would not be able to wear his white or blue dress uniform. It could take days to get another cover by mail. So early on, I got into the habit of checking the hat rack often when I was in the club.

As I have said previously, I have never been much of a drinker. Rather, I went to the O'Club for the comradeship of my peers. I usually drank soft drinks, but I would have an occasional beer or scotch and water. I wasn't a prude; I just didn't like getting drunk.

The nurses and the pilots were in one corner of the bar area, and the security officers sat in another area. Most of the student Air Force security officers were unmarried, so the men looked with great yearning (and lust) at the nurses.

After drinking mass quantities of soft drinks, I needed to use the head (Men's Room) so I checked the hat rack in the lobby, and started for the men's room when I was stopped by an Air Force brigadier general, who was also in uniform. The device that designates the rank of a brigadier general is – ONE STAR – hence they are also known as "one star generals."

Naval officers are divided into two primary categories; line officers and staff officers. Line officers (including LDO security officers) wear a single star above their rank devices (stripes) to denote their status as line officers. The star on a naval officer's dress blue sleeves or shoulder boards has nothing to do with the rank of the officer. But the Air Force general (mainly because of my age and premature grey hair) mistook me for a rear admiral. I even went so far as to say (twice) that I was an Ensign. Evidently, the general wasn't familiar with the rank of ensign and continued to believe that he was talking with a Navy admiral.

The general gave me his business card saying, "If you need anything while you are at Lackland, please give me a call." During the conversation, I had mentioned that I was going into the restaurant for dinner. The general called the O'Club manager and directed him to provide me with "every courtesy."

The manager escorted me to a table in the restaurant. There were only a few people dinning at that early hour. But suddenly, every waitress in the restaurant was standing at my table to take my food order, fill my water glass, and to ensure that I was getting "every courtesy."

A classmate saw the activity at my table and asked, "What's going on?"

When I told him what happened, my classmate returned to the bar and told the rest of the class. Of course, they had to see for themselves, so they came into the dining room, pulled some tables together, and watched the O'Club staff provide me with "every courtesy." When I finished my meal, I paid the bill and went back into the bar, followed shortly thereafter by my classmates.

One of my classmates, a young Air Force officer, declared that as of that moment, he was the Admiral's Aide. He went over to the nurses, one by one, and whispered in their ears. Shortly thereafter, the nurse that he had talked to would come over to the postage- stamp-sized table and join the group of Security Officers. After a half hour or so, the nurses were sitting with the Security Officers, and the pilots were left to wonder what in the hell had happened. By then, it was the pilots who were sitting by themselves.

It must herein be said that I <u>NEVER </u>told any of the nurses that I was an admiral. But my self-appointed Aide did. In fact, he told each nurse, as he whispered in her ear, "the admiral would like to meet you."

The last nurse to join the group sat down, took one look at me, and said, "You're not an admiral." (Her brother was a naval officer.)

"No, I'm not an admiral, but let me tell you how I have come to be called the Lackland Admiral."

All the nurses laughed at the retelling of the story. They decided then and there that I really was "The Lackland Admiral." The nurses were attending classes together at Wilford Hall. When they heard that we were all in the same security class, the two groups became inextricably linked. We enjoyed our time together during the next few weeks.

Chapter 5.5 Happy Birthday…

The naval officers had two other classes to attend over the couple of months that we were to be at Lackland AFB. Since there was a week between classes, the naval officers had a wonderful break. My wife, Pat, traveled to Lackland for a weekend during one of the breaks. However, because of base restrictions, we could not stay in my room at the BOQ, (Bachelor Officer's Quarters) so we stayed in a hotel off base.

I had to go to the BOQ early each morning to mess up the bed and towels to make it appear that I had stayed in the room overnight. I would have automatically lost the room after three days of non-use. While Pat and I were messing up the room on July 6th, several nurses knocked on the door, one after the other, presenting me with birthday cards. After three or four nurses, Pat wasn't so sure that birthday greetings were the only thing going on. To this day, I don't know what she really believes happened between the two classes, but she has no reason to be so suspicious.

Chapter 5.6 Persona non Grata

One of my Air Force classmates wrote his version of the Lackland Admiral story and posted it in the classroom. Everyone, including some of the instructors, started calling me "admiral." That actually worked to my disadvantage.

There was one particular instructor, an Air Force Captain, whom I wanted to take out to dinner. Yes, she was good looking and she was unmarried. She was smart too! And she had some unique security experiences in the field, which was why she was an instructor. I wanted to know more about those first hand experiences, and yes, I wanted to get to know her better.

When I asked her to dinner, she coldly looked at me and said something rather derogatory about my reputation with the nurses. We never went to dinner.

We never met except in class, and she never would talk to me, not even to call on me in class. The Lackland Admiral was definitely **persona non grata**.

We completed our training at Lackland AFB, and then went to the LDO/CWO Officer Indoctrination School, more commonly known in the Navy as "knife and fork school," in Pensacola, Florida. That's where we were supposed to learn how to act like "officers and gentlemen."

CHAPTER SIX

Chapter 6.1 Naval Station Roosevelt Roads, Puerto Rico

(September 1981)

I caught an early morning flight from Pensacola to Miami where I waited several hours to board a plane for Puerto Rico. I arrived in San Juan about five in the afternoon where a chief and a senior chief from the naval station security department met me and took me to the naval station. By the time we got to Roosy Roads, about an hour's drive, I was dead tired.

It was Thursday of the first week in September of 1981. Newly arriving personnel were required to sign in at an office at the front gate. While I was signing in, a commander came into the office asking if I was the new security officer.

"Yes, sir, I am," I responded.

The commander, who was the Command Duty Officer (CDO), reported that the admiral and his official party were being held hostage on the admiral's barge[17] between Roosy Roads and the Island of Vieques.

I thought he was kidding and said, "Tell someone who gives a damn. Just point me to the BOQ. I'm going to bed."

---

17 The term barge mean's a type of boat used by admirals. Similarly, a gig is a boat assigned to shipboard Commanding Officers.

Everyone in the office looked at me in shock. First, ensigns don't talk like that to commanders. Secondly, security officers are supposed to care when the most senior naval officer in the area is being held hostage.

Still, I thought that he was putting me on. What were the chances that a hostage situation would occur at the very moment I arrived at Roosy Roads? Evidently the chances were better than expected.

A hostage situation is one of the more challenging incidents to resolve without someone getting hurt or killed. A hostage situation at sea is made more difficult because there is no way to approach the hostage-takers without being seen, unless you approach from under the water using rebreathing gear. Even SCUBA gear will generate telltale bubbles giving away the presence of responders. I had no idea what resources the security department had for a hostage situation at sea. The answer was – none.

The word "hostage" used to describe this incident was a bit of an overstatement. Yes, the admiral and his party were being detained at sea against their will. Yes, the admiral's barge had been disabled. But the so called hostage-takers were not terrorists, at least not yet. And I wanted to keep it that way.

The hostage-takers were fishermen from Vieques, who were simply demonstrating against the U.S. Navy, which controlled two thirds of the small island. The Navy used the island as a bombing range and a weapons facility to store munitions.

Neither the commanding officer nor the executive officer was on the naval station. Fortunately, there was a SEAL team permanently assigned at Roosy, and they had their own boats and weapons. I encouraged the CDO to call the SEAL team Officer-in- Charge and arrange for the team to rescue the admiral and his party. I also suggested that he tell the SEALs that the use of deadly force was not authorized unless they were attacked.

The SEALs went out to the admiral's barge, chased off the fisher-men, unfouled the screw,[18] and escorted the official party to the local elementary school on Vieques, where the admiral was to inaugurate a local chapter of Sea Cadets.

The situation at the elementary school turned ugly. Demonstrators became violent, knocking over tables, kids, and bystanders. The SEALs rushed the official party to the Naval Weapons Depot where they boarded the boats for the trip back to Roosy Roads.

But the demonstrators had erred. By attacking the kids who were to be inducted into the Sea Cadets, they angered parents and school officials and so they lost support for their cause against the Navy. The anger continued for several days, and I was notified by the Office of the Governor that we might be needed to help quell a riot on Vieques. The riot did not occur. But a storm was definitely brewing.

I finally got to the BOQ and fell into bed. I didn't even bother to unpack. The next day, Tropical Storm Floyd hit the island with fero-cious winds. Security police went around to the residents on the naval station asking them to secure all loose materials such as trash cans and patio furniture. There were a number of damages requiring a po-lice response, including some flooding, but overall, Tropical Storm Floyd exacted relatively minor damage and few injuries on the naval base. Some Puerto Rican communities were not so fortunate.

Between the hostage situation and the storm, I got very little sleep that first weekend. I met the commanding officer and executive of-ficer, a Commander (soon to be Captain) on Monday. Tropical Storm Gert hit the island on Tuesday.

Again, security department personnel worked around the clock, and again, the station sustained little in the way of damage and

_____

18 A screw in Navy-speak is the propeller of a boat or ship.

personnel injury. However, I wondered if the tempo of activity was going to be the everyday fare.

Pat and the boys arrived a month later. Our quarters in junior officer housing had been selected by the security department chiefs. They had decided that I would not want to live next to the executive officer in quarters that were located on a bluff overlooking the ocean. Wrong! Junior officer quarters were in a depression, a low point in the housing area, so there was little in the way of ventilation. Ocean breezes flowed above the depressed area. But like the other junior officers, we made do. However, the issue would resurface again a year or so later.

Soon after my arrival at Roosy Roads, the captain called to say that he had a problem on Vieques: Someone or some group was killing and butchering local cattle. I was to go to Vieques and find out who was butchering their cattle. The culprit turned out to be a civilian guard employed by the Navy who was also an island resident. The guard was fired. What the cattle-owners did with the rustler, if anything, I never found out.

Although terrorist incidents occurred in Puerto Rico, they were mainly directed towards electrical power lines and remote electrical distribution systems near San Juan. Few people on the base took terrorism seriously. As the base security officer, I was concerned that there were no planned strategies and no tactical training for a response to acts of terrorism. There wasn't even an Emergency Operations Center (EOC) from which to direct response operations. The biggest concern seemed to be catching Puerto Ricans who entered the naval station unlawfully for the purpose of poaching land crabs from the relatively undisturbed jungles on the base.

Chapter 6.2 The Land Crab Incident

(September 1981)

I had been on the island about a week. As I drove to the office one weekday morning, the police dispatcher radioed that intruders had been spotted in the jungles behind the CO's office. I drove to the area and helped pursue two men. Although the poachers ran at the sight of the police, they did not resist arrest when security personnel finally caught up with them. I ended up with a large bag of land crabs that the poachers had collected, and which would be used as evidence of their wrongdoing.

I placed the bag of crabs in my police truck. The poachers were placed in a separate police vehicle to be transported to the security office. Just as we were leaving the area, the dispatcher called saying that the naval station CO wanted to see me in his office. When I arrived, the captain said that he wanted me to let the poachers go. They were to be escorted off of the base and no report was to be filed. I was angry, but of course I had no say in the matter. The captain then departed, leaving me standing in the middle of the office with the large bag of land crabs.

I placed the bag of crabs on the captain's desk and returned to my office. About ten minutes later, the captain called, yelling about the land crabs crawling all over his office.

I answered, "What land crabs, sir?"

"You know damn well what land crabs. The crabs you took from the poachers."

"What poachers, sir? We didn't arrest any poachers this morning."

I went to the captain's office and retrieved the land crabs, returning them to the jungles behind the building. The land crab incident was the last time the captain interceded in an apprehension.

Chapter 6.3 Sex in the Single Officers Quarters

(September 1981)

Two days after the land crab incident, I was again called to the CO's office. The captain and the Catholic Chaplain were quietly talking when I entered. The captain ordered me to put an end to promiscuous sex in the Single Officers Quarters (SOQ). Although it was against the rules for enlisted personnel to have women in the barracks, there was no such prohibition in the SOQ.

I answered, "Sir, I am your law enforcement officer, not your morals officer. Sex is not against the law—yet. Morals fall under the purview of the chaplain."

The captain and the chaplain just stood there looking at me. After several uncomfortable moments of silence, I returned to my office in a bunker down the hill. Neither the captain nor the chaplain attempted to stop me, and nothing was ever again said about my stopping promiscuous sex in the Single Officers Quarters.

Chapter 6.4 Missile Movement

(November 1981)

I never expected to provide security for a missile movement. It was on that premise that I had approached the instructors at Lackland Air Force Base, asking them to allow the naval officers to play the role of terrorists. But early on in my assignment at Roosevelt Roads, I was informed that there would be a missile movement, moving *simulated* nuclear missiles from the weapons bunkers to a Navy ship that was tied to the Roosy Roads pier.

The pier was several miles away from the weapons area, and initially the topography favored the terrorists because the weapons area was located in densely foliated jungles. This was to be a graded exercise that would determine the naval station's ability to protect nuclear missiles from an attack by terrorists. The role of the terrorists was to be played by SEAL Team Six, our nation's premier military counterterrorism team.

I drew up a plan based on what I had learned at Lackland. The response plan required a helicopter in addition to the security personnel on the ground. Although the weapons personnel had practiced moving missiles before, they had never gone up against a truly motivated, well-trained, and well-equipped force like SEAL Team Six.

About a week prior to the exercise, I met with the Convoy Commander, a warrant officer, and weapons expert, who was willing to implement new (non-Navy) ideas for the security of the missiles. With his cooperation, I explained the mission and the methods by which we might be able to defeat an aggressor, even one as good as the SEAL Team. The Weapons Department personnel, police, and Marines were eager to learn. They knew well the reputation of the SEALs and they didn't want to lose a missile in transit. They too were motivated.

Prior to the exercise, the security police, Weapons personnel, and Marines drilled the new defensive procedures every day. Several security police officers were selected to fly in the helicopter, which would provide an overhead observation platform, radio communications, and a platform for automatic weapons fire, if needed. I also implemented special codes for use on the radios so that we would not give away our planned tactics to unauthorized listeners.

On the day of the exercise, the Weapons Department personnel loaded the dummy missiles on special trailers. Convoy security was the primary responsibility of the armed Weapons Department personnel. The Marines provided security for the weapons area. The base police would provide traffic control once the convoy got onto the paved roads outside the jungles. The police were also the immediate responders in case of an attack. I believed that the attack would come while the convoy was still in the jungles. Not even SEALs would want to give up cover and concealment for the open ground. Sure enough, that's where the attack took place.

A helicopter had never been used at Roosy Roads to help protect a weapons convoy. The pilot was instructed to remain as high as possible so as not to call attention to the fact that the helicopter was working with the convoy. From that position, they were to provide information as to what was going on around the convoy. They were the convoy's eyes.

The helo crew observed the SEALs approaching the convoy through the jungles, and radioed the information to the Convoy Commander who placed the convoy in a defensive mode. Marines and Weapons Department personnel took up defensive positions under the vehicles and in the jungles to repel the attack. The helicopter descended to an altitude where they could effectively open fire on the SEALs. The combined firepower of the Marines, Weapons Personnel, responding security police, and the helicopter was enough. The SEALs determined that so much firepower would have defeated a well-armed aggressor force of their size. The exercise was over. We had passed the test!

I later called the instructors at Lackland AFB and thanked them for the strategies and tactics they had taught, and which the Air Force commonly used to move missiles across the country. It was effective.

As a result of the drill, I was sent to Nuclear Weapons Security Officer School in Norfolk, Virginia, after which I was then designated as the naval station's Nuclear Weapons Security Officer. So much for the mistaken idea that I would never ever have to provide missile movement security in the Navy.

Chapter 6.5 Savage Monkeys – Sex in the jungle

(March 1982)

The security department senior chief observed a male and female patrol officer drive into the jungle, where they parked and had sex in one of the two police vehicles. They did it again the following night. So the senior chief put out the word that there were savage monkeys in the jungles. I don't know why he chose that scenario.

He also instructed patrol personnel to keep windows rolled up and to patrol jungle roads without stopping. Rumors of monkey attacks abounded throughout the department. Some police officers swore they had actually seen the frightful animals.

About a week later, the senior chief observed the same two officers having sex in a police vehicle at their normal jungle rendezvous. He was in a tree above them. He started making monkey sounds, and then dropped a coconut into the bed of the security pickup truck. The sound of the coconut hitting the truck bed caused the two police officers to believe that they were being attacked. They hastily abandoned their truck while trying to pull up their cammies, which were down around their ankles, draw their weapons, and locate the attacking monkeys.

The senior chief, trying very hard not to laugh, slid down the tree and ordered the police officers to get back to their respective patrol areas. He also ordered them to report to me at 0730. Then the senior chief called me by phone and explained the situation. He couldn't stop laughing.

The police officers were unmarried, and the sex had obviously been consensual, so I decided not to send them to Captain's Mast for dereliction of duty. Instead, I put one police officer on the day watch and the other police officer on the midnight watch with different days off for the rest of their tour at Roosy. It would be a long time before they would get see each other on duty again.

Chapter 6.6 Training Blanco

(June 1982)

The CO's true love was a pure white German shepherd named Blanco. At 75 or 80 pounds, Blanco had the body of a fully- developed adult dog and the mind of a puppy.

He was a big baby, and he loved to play. Like many German shepherds, Blanco tended to growl when he played, so most people gave Blanco a wide berth. He looked and sounded ferocious, but as long as he was playing, he was all bluff. But of course you had to get to know Blanco in order to tell when he was being playful or when he was serious about protecting his fiefdom.

The captain often took the dog to work where Blanco would prowl the offices. He would greet people by jumping up, and placing his substantial paws on their shoulders, licking their faces, and putting his cold wet nose against the visitor's nose. It scared the hell out of the visitors, some of whom were very influential government officials and others who were senior naval officers.

I was raised around German shepherds, so I knew when Blanco was playing and when he was protecting his turf. We became fast friends because I always took the time to play.

I correctly guessed that there would be a time when I would have to go to the captain's quarters in the middle of the night, and I didn't want to have to fight him off. Anytime he saw me on the base, it was play time and I did nothing to discourage that.

The captain stopped by my office one day, and took a while to get to the point. Finally, he said that he wanted the security department's canine unit to train Blanco.

"What type of training do you want?" I asked.

The captain opined as how he wanted Blanco to walk at his side, to heel, sit, and lay down on command, especially when he was on a leash. Also, he wanted Blanco to stop jumping on people.

"Sir," I answered, "we train dog teams. That's the dog and the handler. If we train your dog, you have to be with him."

That wasn't what the captain wanted to hear. He looked at me with hard eyes, which eventually softened. "When can we begin?" he asked.

"Saturday morning at 0700," I responded.

At 0700 on the next Saturday morning, Blanco and the captain arrived at the chain-link fenced canine training area. The military working dog handler went over some of the basic rules for working with a dog while in training. This was work time, not play time. The captain's voice was to be measured except when praising the dog. The handler started with "heel." Blanco wanted to play. He wouldn't listen to the captain.

I took Blanco and worked with him for about five minutes. Blanco was walking at the heel position like a champion. The captain took the leash and Blanco refused to listen to him. He pulled on the leash and whined. As far as Blanco was concerned, anytime the captain held the leash, it was playtime.

I continued to work with Blanco in the weeks that followed, usually without a leash on the front lawn of the CO's house. He made real progress, but only with me.

The captain never again returned to the Military Working Dog training area with Blanco. When I asked him why, he said, "I just can't bring myself to talk to Blanco in a cross manner."

Here was a senior naval officer whose professional life depended on discipline, but who could not bring himself to do the things necessary to instill discipline in his canine buddy. Unrealized by anyone at the time, that lack of canine discipline would create an incident during a visit by the Chief of Naval Operations (CNO).

Naval Station Roosevelt Roads Security Department Bunker
The Canine Unit was housed on top of the bunker
(Photo by John Cline)

Chapter 6.7 High Tea with the CNO's Wife

Winter in Washington D.C. can be cold. Puerto Rico was a favorite destination for Members of Congress, senior administration officials, and senior military officers who wanted to get away from the wintery conditions of the eastern seaboard. The Chief of Naval Operations, who is the senior uniformed officer in the Navy, decided to pay an official visit to Naval Station Roosevelt Roads. He took his wife. (Smart man!)

While the commanding officer planned briefings for the CNO, the captain's wife began planning a "tea" for the wife of the CNO. The captain's wife called a meeting of the officer's wives.

She made assignments and gave instructions regarding how the wives should dress, what times they would arrive (based upon the rank of their husbands), and even what conversations were appropriate and inappropriate. This was to be an informal affair.

The fact that my wife worked at the commissary and should have been at work when the tea was to be held didn't faze the CO's wife for a moment. She gave Patsy orders and expected that those orders would be carried out without question. Patsy informed her boss that she wouldn't be at work on the appointed day. Her boss, a Lieutenant Commander, fully understood.

Patsy was assigned to help the captain's wife prepare the "good" china that had never been unpacked following the CO's move to Puerto Rico. On the morning that the tea was to take place, each piece of china had to be unwrapped, washed, and set in its proper place. The captain's wife determined the proper place for each item. She fussed over each little element of the setting. Finally the ladies started to arrive (by order of rank) at the captain's quarters. The CNO's wife would be the last to arrive, as dictated by military protocol. With the ladies properly seated, waiting for the CNO's wife, everything was in perfect readiness. The captain's wife would not tolerate anything less. Minutes before the CNO's wife was to arrive, disaster struck.

The disaster had a name: Blanco! He was delighted to see all of the beautifully dressed and well-coiffed ladies sitting down where he could say hello in his typical doggy fashion. He jumped on each lady, placed his paws on their sun-dresses, and licked their faces. Those who were standing were not exempt; he jumped up and placed his paws on their shoulders and tried to lick their faces too. Of course, he growled too.

The ladies did not know Blanco. As far as they were concerned, the dog was attacking them. And so they did what ladies almost always do when attacked: They screamed and ran.

The captain's wife tried to get Blanco under control, but by now, chasing and growling at the running, screaming ladies was a fabulous game. The more the women screamed and ran, the more he chased and growled. He paid absolutely no attention to the captain's wife who kept screaming his name in her failed attempt to lock him away in another room. One swoop of his enormous tail cleared the tea setting from of the coffee table in front of the couch where the CNO's wife was to sit. The interior of the house and the tea setting looked like it had been struck by a small tornado.

The CNO's wife was expected at any moment. The captain's wife yelled for Pat to call me. Patsy called the police dispatcher. I was elsewhere on the base. The dispatcher called me on the radio and said that there was an emergency at the CO's quarters and that the CO's wife wanted me to personally respond to the situation. Expecting the worst, I turned on the lights and siren and raced for the CO's quarters. My heart was pounding because I knew that Patsy was there.

As I arrived in front of the white two-story house, I saw women running across the lawn away from the building. Some women jumped into their cars.

Others kept running down the street, probably toward their own quarters. I cautiously entered the front door with my hand on my pistol. The ladies pointed to the captain's wife. She said, "John, take control of the dog."

Blanco was still running around the house, chasing the few women who remained. I intercepted him, grabbed his collar, and told him "heel." He walked out of the house like a true gentleman, with his head held high. I placed him in the front seat of the police truck (locally known as the War Wagon). He looked at the ladies on the front lawn and whined. He still wanted to play.

Most of the ladies returned to the captain's quarters. They hurriedly replaced the tea setting and put the interior of the house back into an acceptable order. The CNO's wife arrived and expressed regret for having been delayed. The captain's wife audibly sighed. Blanco spent the rest of the day with me.

Chapter 6.8 Fiestas Patronales

(July 1982)

Held to honor a town or city's patron saint, fiestas patronales are extremely popular annual festivities that take place in the town square. The festivities include processions, games, some of which look more like gambling, rides, musical shows, and local foods. The executive officer called me one afternoon in July saying that the City of Fajardo was holding its festival in honor of its patron saint, Santiago Apostol, and that the captain, officers, and enlisted personnel were cordially invited to attend festivities that evening.

Cordially invited in the Navy is a code for you had "better be there." Fajardo was a city of about 40,000 people, and anti-Navy sentiment at that time was fairly high. We would be in summer dress white uniforms. What wonderful targets we would make!

I contacted the Senior NIS Agent and asked if NIS could provide protective services for the CO.

"Sure" he said, "but you will have to submit a request in writing to Washington D.C. before we can begin such a detail."

The festival was to start in a couple of hours. I returned to the office and put together a protective detail using security personnel. We had no authority off the base, but I wasn't going to allow the CO and his wife to become a target.

We only had a few military police officers who spoke even a little Spanish. The few that we had were asked to dress in civilian clothes. Their job was to walk around with the crowd, staying in separate quadrants of the square, and listen to conversations to determine whether there was a threat to the senior officer personnel and their spouses.

I assigned our Puerto Rican military working dog handler to be the CO's driver. His job was to keep us in sight as we walked around the square. A chase car contained four heavily armed military police officers. At best, the cars were about twenty five yards away. At worst, there was a 100 yard separation between the CO, and his wife, and the XO and his wife, and the car. Security personnel had radios with ear pieces.

For about two hours, everyone except for the security detail was having fun. Suddenly a group of locals who had been drinking heavily, gathered together to confront the CO. They started toward their target with one of our Spanish speaking security police officers nearby. He reported that the group was definitely going for the CO.

I asked the CO and his wife to get in the car. The captain said to take the wives back to Roosy, but that he and the XO would stay and continue playing the games at booths set up in the square.

The car was as close as it could get. Police officers in the chase car set up a zone of protection. The two wives immediately went to the car. I placed a control hold on the CO, lifted him onto his toes, and walked him to the car where I placed him inside and doubled him up on the floor so that he could not be seen from outside the car.

The XO had once asked me what I would do to protect him. I had told him that my primary objective was to protect the captain. If the XO was nearby, we would offer him the same level of protection. But if he fell behind, he would be left behind. I don't think he believed me. He was trying to get in the car when I ordered the driver to go. The XO had a very difficult time getting into the accelerating car, but he made it – barely. We almost left him lying in the street.

There was no conversation during the ride back to Naval Station Roosevelt Roads except for radio calls to the chase car behind us and to the front gate on the base. We drove the captain to his quarters without stopping at the gate. I walked with the CO and his wife to the front door.

The captain turned and looked me in the eye and said, "I just want to know one thing. How can a skinny guy like you pick me up and stuff me in a car?"

The captain was over six feet tall and weighed about 250 pounds. I smiled. "Trade secret."

Nothing more was said about my manhandling the captain. We drove the XO and his wife to their quarters. With the captain gone from the festival, the group of locals chose not to confront any of the remaining naval personnel. I firmly believe that we prevented a dangerous situation from occurring that evening.

Chapter 6.9 Barring the Captain's Daughter

(April 1983)

Each spring and summer, military dependents who attended colleges and universities returned to the base in Puerto Rico. After a night of partying, the captain's daughter returned to the CO's quarters and told Blanco to sic the civilian armed guard who was patrolling the grounds around the quarters. The guard was there specifically to protect the captain and his family.

Blanco growled and took off after the guard. The guard could have shot the dog, but decided instead to climb up a palm tree and call for assistance on his radio. Blanco was returned to the house, and the daughter was detained by the police while an investigation report was generated.

The next morning, the captain read the report. He looked at me and asked what I thought he should do. I asked him what he would do if it was someone else's dependent. He said that he would bar them from the base for a year.

I said nothing.

He looked up at me from behind his desk and said, "Jeez, John, you're asking me to bar my own daughter."

"No, sir, I'm not. But if you don't, you have no moral standing to bar anyone else."

Early the next morning, the captain took his daughter to the airport in San Juan. The captain's wife never forgave me. She never talked to me again. She didn't call me when Blanco acted up, and she didn't talk to me months later when I took the family to the airport for their return to the states when the CO transferred to his next duty assignment.

Chapter 6.10 Anti and Counterterrorism Training

(May 1983)

Someone at NIS/NCIS in Washington D.C. developed a curriculum that was "recommended" for commanding and executive officers. It fell to the various security officers to provide the instruction to the CO and XO through a series of briefings.

The counterterrorism training discussed strategies and tactics tailored to the individual ship or station. Antiterrorism, on the other hand, were measures that a ship or station could take to prevent terrorism. Those procedures were much more general in nature. Counterterrorism and antiterrorism required training and money that had not been budgeted.

Getting on the calendars of the CO and XO for anti and counterterrorism training was nearly impossible. I never did get to brief the captain. So I decided to take a more direct approach with the XO.

After having been told several times to "get on the XO's calendar," only to have our meetings cancelled at the last minute, I went to the XO's office. He looked up and said, "Sorry John, I had to cancel again."

I climbed up on his desk and sat cross-legged. He looked at me as if I had gone mad.

I said, "Sir, I understand that you are a very busy man. Please don't mind me, go ahead with your work."

The XO went back to his reading—and continued to read for about five minutes. Then he looked at me and said, "You're not going away, are you?"

"No, sir," I answered, "but you just go ahead with your work, I'll be here when you're finished."

Thank God, the XO had a sense of humor. After fidgeting for a while, he put down his paperwork and accepted the first forty- five minute briefing.

There were a series of six briefings. We went through one brief-ing each week for six weeks. After each briefing, I wrote a memo that indicated what training had been accomplished. I personally took the memo to the personnel office where the memo was placed in the XO's service record. Everybody, including the personnel officer, thought that the training and the memo were a complete waste of time.

Some months later, after he had rotated to his next assignment, the former XO called on the phone. He was excited. He said that he had been "selected to be the next commanding officer at U.S. Naval Base Sigonella in Italy." Then he said, "It's all because of you. They said I was a "Ready Round," because I had the antiterrorism training that a CO would need in an area where terrorism was fairly commonplace."

After he had been the CO at Sigonella for about a year, I got an-other afternoon call from the former XO.

This time, he was yelling into the phone saying, "I knew what to do – I knew what to do."

Here's what had happened.

U.S. Intelligence determined that Abu Abbas, the convicted Palestinian terrorist who masterminded the 1985 hijacking of the Italian cruise liner *Achille Lauro*, was being flown to freedom after surrendering to Egyptian authorities following the hijacking. During the hijacking, Jews had been separated from the rest of the passen-gers, and sixty-nine year old Leon Klinghoffer, a retiree and wheel-chair-ridden stroke victim, was shot and dumped overboard in front of his wife. He was an American citizen.

President Reagan ordered Navy Tomcats from the *USS Saratoga* to force Egyptian flight 2843 to land on the U.S. side of the NATO base at Sigonella, Italy, where our former XO was in command.

The scenario had been covered in those dreaded antiterrorism briefings. It didn't hurt that he had SEAL Team Six to surround the aircraft and to apprehend the terrorists. SEAL Team Six was an eighty man unit, and at that time, it was our most elite military counterterrorism unit. But Abu Abbas was holding the ultimate trump card. He had been given diplomatic immunity and a diplomat's passport by the Egyptian government.

It's ironic that the four terrorists were flying with diplomatic passports, and that ten armed members of Force 777, Egypt's elite counterterrorism unit, was protecting the terrorists. Abu Abbas was turned over to the Italian Government, who released him because of his diplomatic immunity.

The captain was mentally ready to handle a potentially dangerous situation thrust upon him out of the blue. He knew what to do. He was prominently mentioned in Tom Clancy's book, Shadow Warriors.

Chapter 6.11 WASP Boats (Waterborne Antiterrorism Security Police Boats)

Naval Station Roosevelt Roads was vulnerable to an attack from sea. Other than a tug boat under the control of the Water Front Operations Department, the naval station had no patrol boats or sea-going weapons platforms with which to repel a terrorist attack.

AIRLANT, The Commander, Naval Air Force, Atlantic, and the parent organization of the naval station, was willing to fund a couple of patrol boats. But which boats? We looked at new readily available models, but could find nothing that would meet our needs.

Paul Hureau from Boston Whaler came to Roosevelt Roads to see what we needed. With Paul, the staff at AIRLANT, and our people, we finally settled on the requirements for a patrol boat that went out to bid. While we believed that we needed a forty foot boat to maneuver in the rough seas around Puerto Rico and the Virgin Islands, our perceived needs were put aside for cost constraints.

They were also put aside for the purpose of hiding the cost of the patrol boats from congressional scrutiny. There weren't many forty foot patrol boats in the Navy, so a new acquisition would be easily recognized by congressional staffers who were always looking for ways to reduce the military budget. We had to settle on a twenty-eight foot boat, the size of which was plentiful in the Navy's inventory. That's the story that the budget people told me, anyway.

Boston Whaler's Commercial Division built the Ramo Raider from an existing design, that of the Boston Whaler Outrage. They beefed up the Outrage to handle the rigors of the Caribbean and our anti-drug and antiterrorism mission.

Someone on a staff in Washington D.C. wrote a requirement that the boat had to be cut in half and still be able to float and to maintain a firefight for thirty minutes.

The Ramo Raider prototype went to the SEALs who took the boat to the Pawtuxet River, cut it two, and simulated a sustained firefight for at least thirty minutes. It floated and it survived!

A year or so later, we received two Ramo Raiders. A senior chief boatswain mate with patrol boat experience in Viet Nam was selected to be the WASP Boat division chief.

Several people from the naval station were chosen to serve on the boats; about half of the boat crews were women. He trained his personnel based on his experiences in Nam. The boats had two M-60's and two 50 caliber machine guns. The crews became so proficient in

SEA STORIES AND NAVY TALES

shooting the weapons, that they got me in trouble with Captain Bill Mackey, the Commanding Officer of VC-8.

VC-8 helicopter crews tossed 50 gallon barrels out of helicopters for use as targets. Our crews began firing closer and closer to the aircraft instead of waiting until the barrels hit the water. That prompted a call from Captain Mackey who said it was getting difficult to find pilots and crews who would fly the target mission. I promised that we would wait for the barrels to hit the water before firing. Then I contacted the senior chief and we had a rather terse discussion.

U.S. Air Force photograph - Air Force Master
Sergeants Reenlisting on a WASP Boat

The senior chief's favorite maneuver was to toss a visitor into the sea by centrifugal force during a tight turn. He once attempted to toss me out, but forewarned, I hung on. Some Air Force pilots were interested in the boats and asked to go for a short spin. The senior chief took them out and promptly dumped them into the sea. They said that the turn was the equivalent of about six Gs. I wouldn't know about that, but the senior chief was good at dumping first time visitors, regardless of rank or position.

The WASP crews were very well trained and they were expert in their patrol duties. Too good! During an exercise in which SEALs were again the good guys, with a mission to provide reconnaissance for the military force attacking from sea, the WASP crew spotted the SEALs about sundown, swimming underwater toward Roosy Roads. The SEALs were supposed to say a code word so that the waterborne police officers would know that they were part of the exercise and let them through. For whatever reason, the SEALs never gave the password, so the WASP patrol continued to pursue them. The SEALs made it to a small island about a quarter mile from the base. They were bottled-up there until the exercise was ended.

Photographer Unknown Airborne Ramo Raider in Saudi Arabia

I thought the WASP crews would get credit for their good work. Quite the opposite occurred. Congressmen had been invited guests during the exercise. When they got back to Washington D.C., they asked the question, "Why are we spending so much money on SEALs when the police can bottle them up and render them ineffective?"

I got my butt chewed by an old acquaintance who was a Special Warfare Navy Captain assigned to the Pentagon. I refused to pass the ass-chewing on to the WASP crews. They were good at their jobs. Bravo Zulu (Navy-speak for Well Done) WASP Crews.

Toward the end of my tour at Roosevelt Roads, we were visited by an inspection team that was to evaluate the effectiveness of the WASP boats and crews. The inspectors laid out a course that took them south along the shoreline of Puerto Rico, then across to St. Thomas in the Virgin Islands, and back again to Roosy Roads. It was a stormy day with ten and twelve foot swells.

The inspectors got violently seasick. When they completed the inspection, one of the formal suggestions was that the Navy purchase forty foot patrol boats in order to better handle the seas around Puerto Rico and the Virgin Islands.

About a year after I left Roosy Roads, the security department did get larger boats. I heard that overall, they didn't perform as well as the Ramo Raider, but they did ride better.

Chapter 6.12 New CO's and XO's

Captain Clint Smith became the executive officer of Naval Station Roosevelt Roads. Clint was an exceptional test pilot. I have seen literally hours of film where Clint landed newly designed aircraft without knowing whether the planes could withstand a carrier landing or takeoff. Although he was my boss, he became one of my closest friends.

Not long after Clint took over as XO, the commanding officer received orders to his next duty station. The CO called me to his office and asked me to drive him and his wife to the airport in San Juan because he was concerned that Blanco might bite a baggage handler.

After I dropped off the captain and his wife at the passenger terminal, I took Blanco to be crated and placed on the aircraft. The baggage handlers took one look at Blanco and were more than happy to let me place him in the crate, and to stay with him until it was time to move him to the restricted area. As I walked away, he whined. I really loved that dog, and it broke my heart that I would never see him again. Blanco returned to Roosy Roads when the former captain returned as an admiral. But by then, I had already gone to my next duty station.

Captain Jim Keathley became the Commanding Officer of Naval Station Roosevelt Roads, and a new Rear Admiral arrived to take over as Commander, Naval Forces, Caribbean.

Chapter 6.13 "No Man is an Island"

During a change of command ceremony at the Atlantic Fleet Weapons Training Facility (AFWTF), the admiral, who was to be the principle speaker, was introduced by the outgoing CO as Admiral Diego Garcia. There was muffled laughter by military personnel in the audience. (Diego Garcia is an island in the Indian Ocean.)

The Admiral, whose first name is Diego, rose to the podium where he deftly cited, "I assure you, No man is an island. But I am happy to be here today for this change of command ceremony."

He then went on with his prepared speech.

It's a good thing that the captain who had introduced the admiral was the outgoing commander. He would have been teased mercilessly throughout his tour, had he been the incoming officer.

Chapter 6.14 The Christmas Tree Incident

There are no pine trees in Puerto Rico. Christmas trees, like every other product that is imported to the island, must be transported by ship or by air. The Navy Exchange system only buys so many Christmas trees, so getting a good one is very much dependent on getting to the Navy Exchange (NEX) soon after the trees arrive.

Pat worked at the commissary, which was near the Exchange. One morning about two weeks before Christmas, she noticed Christmas trees in the NEX parking lot. She stopped to see what was available. Most of the trees were in poor shape, but one tree that was leaning against the building was perfect. She bought the tree and immediately took it to our quarters, after which she returned to work at the commissary. That night, she and the boys decorated the tree. It was truly beautiful.

During the Christmas asaltos, the admiral, along with other officers and townspeople came to our quarters where the lighted tree stood in all of its glory. The admiral said, "Nice tree."

I thanked him and told him that Patsy had picked it out. Nothing more was ever said. However, when we went to the admiral's quarters as part of the Christmas asaltos, we noticed that he had a truly gangly "Charlie Brown" Christmas tree. It must have been the last available tree.

Captain Bill Mackey was the VC-8 commanding officer. VC-8 was one of several tenant commands at Naval Station Roosevelt Roads at that time. Years later, Bill told me a slightly different version of the story. Apparently, someone at the NEX, probably the Naval Exchange Officer, had called the admiral when the trees came in, so that the admiral could have first pick.

The admiral selected a tree, which he leaned against the building, but which was away from the other trees that were for sale. He told the Exchange Officer that he would pick up the tree after work. Of course, it wasn't there when he got back hours later.

Captain Mackey said the Admiral called the commanding officers of the various commands asking if they knew who had stolen his Christmas tree. I don't know if he realized who ended up with it. If he recognized it when he visited my quarters during the asaltos, he didn't say anything. But then, the admiral always was a perfect gentleman.

Chapter 6.15 Christmas Asaltos

You may not be familiar with the term "asaltos," meaning to assault. Until I got to Puerto Rico, I certainly wasn't. In Puerto Rico, the Christmas season starts fairly early in December and continues right on through mid-January with the celebration of Three Kings Day.

During that period, if you are lucky, you will be "assaulted" by a group of local citizens who will serenade you with songs of the Christmas season, usually in Spanish. You are then obligated to provide food and drink – rum is always a favorite – to your guests. IT IS FUN!!! And when it's time to move on, you are *expected* to join the group for the rest of the night. The Christmas asaltos often starts early in the evening, while there is still sunlight, and lasts until daylight the next day. Patsy and I never lasted more than a couple of hours.

Not everyone is visited by an asaltos. It is an honor accorded only to the more popular officials and friends of the people who planned the event. Also, you are never told when an asaltos will occur. However, someone always had a musical chime that played a short warning tune so you knew that the asaltos had arrived. Of course, the commanding officer was informed of the arrival of the revelers when they stopped at the main gate, asking for permission to enter the base.

Following the asaltos on our quarters, the ever expanding group went to the captain's quarters. Later, it was decided to assault the quarters of the admiral. Even though tradition says you don't warn the recipient, Billie Keathley, the CO's wife, and the kindest, most gentle soul in the world, snuck off to another room and warned the admiral by phone. The admiral was waiting with a full larder and an adequate supply of rum. The admiral knew how to have fun, and was always a most gracious host.

Chapter 6.16 Taking Care of a Traffic Ticket for My Wife's Boss

Pat likes to tell the story about her boss, a lieutenant commander who at that time was the commissary officer at Roosevelt Roads. Apparently, he had gotten a traffic ticket for failing to stop at the naval station's one and only stop light, and he would have to appear in Traffic Court. I was also the Traffic Court judge.

The commissary officer stopped by and told Pat that he was on the way to have me "take care of his ticket." Patsy says she smiled, but inwardly she was laughing. She knew what would happen.

The Commissary Officer arrived in my office, and after a few minutes of cheerful banter, indicated that he wanted me to "take care of his traffic ticket."

"Sure," I said. "Did you fail to stop at the light?" I asked. "Oh, yes," he said.

"Okay," I said, "I accept your guilty plea and find you guilty and award you three points on your driving record." (Drivers lost their driving privileges at ten points.) He looked a little surprised, but said nothing as he left. When he got back to work, he told Pat the story and she had no sympathy.

"Well, he took care of it, didn't he?" she asked. She still laughs when she tells the story.

Chapter 6.17 Protecting the Admiral

It was questioned whether the admiral required personal protection when he was away from the naval station. There were two schools of thought:

Because he was a senior Puerto Rican naval officer, he would need no additional personal protection in Puerto Rico, unless it was from the sizeable number of women who would have liked to become his next wife. The admiral's wife of many years had died a few years earlier.

The admiral did require personal protection because he represented the United States, because he was the senior officer on the island, and because he was a high profile public official.

My position was there would be times when it was prudent for the admiral to have additional personal protection. The admiral decided that the Police of Puerto Rico (POPR) would provide any protection he needed when he was off of the base. The first time protection was used, the POPR led the way in a marked police vehicle. The admiral followed in his official car. A few miles down the road, the police car drove off and left the admiral in the dust. They never came back for him. The admiral decided that other arrangements might have to be made.

It was decided that if the event was a high profile event, the NIS would provide protection along with the POPR. If the event to which the admiral was travelling was not high profile, he would drive himself.

On occasion, the security police provided an armed driver and whatever number of armed security personnel that were required. Even though we had no authority off of the base, we had no reason to believe that the POPR would object. NIS probably would object, so we didn't bother to tell them.

Chapter 6.18 Crime Prevention

I met Gary Bjorklund (another BJ) at a gathering of officers during a barbeque. He complained that Puerto Ricans from neighboring towns were going through the housing areas at night and stealing everything that wasn't nailed down. Because we didn't have investigators, we relied on NIS for criminal investigations. All of our police personnel were patrol officers. I spent a couple of nights in BJ's tool shed hoping to catch the thieves. During my stay in the tool shed, I decided to take a more proactive approach regarding thefts in the housing areas.

I asked Captain Keathley for permission to talk with the Alcalde (mayor) of each of the towns that surrounded the naval station. He agreed. I met with the mayors and told them that I didn't want to see any Puerto Rican get hurt on the base, but that I had to do something about the thefts that were occurring. Most of the mayors smiled and said they could sympathize with my dilemma, but that there was little that they could do. One Alcalde, however, took the situation to heart.

The Alcalde is a very influential person within the town or city. Within reason, he was authorized to spend city funds to help pay for food, rent, house payments, or utilities when a family was in dire need. So when the Alcalde speaks, the residents of the town listen. In the case of the city of Naguabo, I'm told the Alcalde called a meeting in the town square. Evidently, the Alcalde told the people of Naguabo that the naval station police were now using attack dogs to patrol the base. We weren't. He continued by saying that anyone who got hurt, or who was apprehended on the base, would not be eligible for public assistance.

For the rest of my tour at Naval Station Roosevelt Roads we did not receive another report of housing area thefts by Puerto Ricans. The two theft reports that we did get were perpetrated by sailors. This might appear coincidental, but just two weeks after I left the island to go to my next duty station, a couple of Puerto Rican intruders entered the Bachelor Officers Quarters, tied up a lieutenant commander, looted his quarters, and then got into a gun fight with an FBI agent who was loading his car in the parking lot outside the BOQ. They got away. Getting the assistance of the Alcalde was true crime prevention.

Chapter 6.19 Becoming a Son of the City of Naguabo (October 1983)

During lunch several months later, the Naguabo Alcalde mentioned that the city was in danger of being fined by the Environmental Protection Agency (EPA) for not having communications between City Hall and the city dump, which was located several miles away.

That evening, I searched through my personally-owned radio gear and found two old radios and a couple of power supplies that I no longer used. I called Johnny Melendez, the assistant mayor, and offered to give him the radios if the city would buy two antennas and the co-axial cable needed to hook up the radios. Johnny accepted the offer, bought the antennas and coaxial cable, and had the radios installed. When the EPA official returned a couple of weeks later, they demonstrated that they could talk between the dump and City Hall. The EPA let them off the hook, saving the city $100,000 that they didn't have. I promptly forgot about the incident.

About a month after the EPA inspection, I was called to the office of the commanding officer. Captain Keathley told me that the City of Naguabo was having some kind of event, and that I was to attend the affair with my wife. Now that was strange. Why was the captain ordering my wife and me to attend a city event? I was ordered to wear my summer white uniform with ribbons.

Patsy and I arrived at the City Plaza, found a place to park, and went to the gazebo in the center of the square in search of Johnny Melendez, the Assistant Mayor. Johnny escorted Patsy and me up the steps of the gazebo and seated us with the Alcalde and the city leaders. There were literally hundreds of people in the square.

The Alcalde got up and spoke into the microphone. His voice carried throughout the square and the people clapped enthusiastically.

Then he called Patsy to the microphone and presented her with a lovely bouquet of flowers. She didn't know why she was being presented flowers, but she thanked the Alcalde and returned to her seat.

Patsy receiving flowers from the Alcalde (Photo by Johnny Melendez)

John receiving a proclamation
(Photo by Johnny Melendez)

I was called to the microphone where the Alcalde continued speaking in Spanish and the crowd went slightly wild. He then presented me with a plaque from the City of Naguabo and turned the microphone over to me to make a few comments.

My Spanish was extremely limited, but I thanked the Alcalde and the residents of the city for this high honor. Then, in English, I apologized for my limited ability to speak Spanish. The crowd laughed, and I returned to my seat somewhat embarrassed. Johnny Melendez explained later that I had been made a son of the City of Naguabo, something they took very seriously. At the time, I didn't realize just how seriously they took the honor.

Chapter 6.20 Being a Son had City Expectations

Around Easter time, the residents of the City of Naguabo line the main street with tables and chairs from their homes. Then they fill the tables with food and drink for an Easter celebration.

It is a time when those sons and daughters of Naguabo and their families who no longer live in the city return for a week of celebration. There are many Puerto Ricans who live throughout the stateside eastern seaboard. Those who are able, return to Naguabo for the celebration.

Patsy and I received an invitation to attend the festivities. I don't like crowds, so I wasn't particularly enthused about the idea, but we got into our little red truck and went to Naguabo. There was a line of vehicles several miles long, and after waiting about an hour, during which we only advanced a few car lengths, I said the hell with it, and we returned to the base to have lunch at the O'Club.

Monday morning, I was called to the CO's office where the Alcalde, assistant Alcalde, chief of police, fire chief, and the city clerk were waiting. They were not happy. My lack of attendance had created somewhat of a local incident.

I explained that I did try to attend the festivities, but that after waiting an hour or so to get into the city square, I gave up and returned to the base. Johnny Melendez translated my excuse in Spanish for the Alcalde, who then turned to the chief of police and started talking to him in machine-gun rapid fire Spanish.

Johnny turned to me and said, "You were not expected to wait in line. You should have driven down the wrong side of the street to the center of town. The Alcalde had a parking place for you and had chairs set up for you and Patsy next to him."

I really felt bad for not sticking it out. But I would never have thought to drive down the wrong side of the street to get ahead of the line of waiting residents. I profusely apologized. I was invited to lunch, which I gladly attended.

Never have I been made to feel more welcome than I was by the officials from the city of Naguabo.

Chapter 6.21 Dinner with the XO

(Captain Clint Smith was, and remains, a bit of a prankster.)

Pat went to San Diego for a couple of weeks to be with her parents. Coincidentally, the wives of Lieutenant Jim Adkins and Chaplain Rod Kelley were also in the States.

Clint Smith called me at the office and asked if Jim, Rod, and I would like to have dinner with the Smiths that evening. I accepted and said that I would contact Rod and Jim. Then I asked what the uniform would be for the occasion. There was a silence for more than a few seconds, and then he answered, "Choker whites with medals and swim suits." I contacted Rod (who also likes a good prank) and Jim Adkins, and it was decided that we would go to dinner wearing the uniform dictated by Clint.

We arrived at the appointed time, and as we were standing at the front door, I could see Sue Smith through the window setting the table. We rang the doorbell. Sue looked out of the window and saw the three of us standing there in dress white uniforms. From her vantage point, she could only see the choker whites. Her hand flew to her mouth and her eyes notably widened. She got a really horrified look on her face. She literally ran around the table three times while Clint answered the door.

As soon as Clint saw us in choker whites and swim suits, he broke out laughing and called for Sue to "Come see this." Sue hesitated, probably because she and Clint were dressed casually, but then she came to the front door where she got the whole picture. There was visible relief on her face. Looking at our bare legs, she broke out in laughter and made some comment about skinny legs. We had a great evening of convivial dinning and conversation. But for me, the funniest part of the evening was the look on Sue's face when she thought we were there for a formal dinner.

Chapter 6.22 Rescue at Sea (or don't bother the doctor)

It was late in the afternoon when I got a call from the XO, Captain Clint Smith. A civilian tug boat that had been towing a barge with 100,000 gallons of gasoline was on fire. The tug's crew had abandoned ship off the eastern coast of Puerto Rico within a few miles of the naval station. That presented two problems:

1. There was the potential for a very big explosion, and since the tug and the barge were adrift, that explosion could impact the naval station.

2. The crew was drifting around in a rubber raft and darkness would soon be descending. The crew needed to be rescued soon or they would be carried out to sea where the chances of rescue were greatly diminished. The tug's captain had a hand-held radio which he used to report their position.

Much of the thirty five miles of coastline on Naval Station Roosevelt Roads was undeveloped jungle. So getting to various points where we could look out to sea meant walking through the thick foliage, which slowed our rescue. The sun was about to set and the coastline was not a sandy beach, but rather it was abounded with large boulders with razor sharp edges. The whole operation was fast becoming FUBAR. (Military people will know what FUBAR means.)

Someone spotted the raft with its crewmen bobbing around in the water about a half mile from the shoreline. The tide was shifting. We had no boats in the area, so we did the next best thing: We called the SEALs, but their boats were unavailable.

Who better to swim out and help? Within minutes, four SEALs arrived and carefully made their way into the water avoiding the boulders with razor sharp edges. They swam to the raft and pulled it against the tide to the shoreline. This was no small two-man raft. It was a large ten-man raft with six crewmen. The SEALs, swimming against the tide, did a great job. They appeared to be nearly exhausted when they got near the shoreline. But their problems were just beginning.

The boulders prevented them from getting the raft to a point where we could get the injured crewmen ashore. So the SEALs walked on the boulders, every step resulting in their feet being cut. The crewmen had appropriately removed their shoes before entering the raft, so they too would have cut their feet had they tried walking ashore. Finally, the SEALs found a place where they could safely beach the raft.

There is a certain liability inherent with rescuing people who are the victims of man or nature. The rescuers are expected to provide care to the victims before releasing them on their own recognizance, or to others who will provide additional care. We already had four injured SEALs whose feet were cut. The tug's crew had been burned. I was adamant that the SEALs and the crew of the tug be examined by the hospital's medical staff. Captain Smith agreed.

We wrapped the SEALs' cut feet with bandages from first aid kits and transported the SEALs and the tug's crew to the base hospital. By now it was well after sunset.

The hospital was deserted except for a single corpsman who sat behind a desk in the lobby. We ushered the crew and the SEALs into the lobby, and I asked to see a doctor.

The corpsman answered, "We only have one doctor on duty, and he can't be disturbed."

I ordered him to "call the doctor." He refused.

Captain Smith, who was in civilian clothes, identified himself, and ordered the corpsman to call the doctor. The corpsman again refused. By now I was angry. The corpsman threatened to call the police. I said, "I am the (expletive) police; now call the doctor." The corpsman called the doctor, whispering something into the phone that I couldn't hear.

It turned out that the doctor had been sleeping. He rubbed the sleep out of his eyes as he walked into the lobby. He wasn't happy about having his nap interrupted and he said so. I explained the situation and asked him to examine the SEALs and the crew of the tug. He refused. Captain Smith identified himself by stating his rank and position and ordered the doctor to perform the necessary examinations. The doctor refused. I explained that the SEALs were Navy personnel and that it was his duty to examine them.

Still the doctor again refused saying, "Have them come back during sick call."

The XO asked to use the phone to call the hospital's commanding officer. The corpsman refused to allow the XO to use the phone. I got on the radio and asked the dispatcher to contact the hospital's CO at his quarters.

It was then that the doctor said, "Okay, I'll examine the SEALs, but each of the tug's crew will have to have $35 dollars in hand before I will examine them."

Both the XO and I were way beyond angry. I guess the doctor finally decided it wasn't worth the stress, so he examined the SEALs, patched up their wounds, and then examined the tug's crewmen. Several of the crew had been badly burned. In fact, the crewmen didn't want us to touch them because they were afraid their skin would fall off.

We released the crew to tug boat association officials, who indicated they would get medical care for the crew in San Juan. I was deeply offended by the performance of the Navy doctor and corpsman.

Chapter 6.23 More Adventures with the Base Hospital Staff

A small minority of the medical staff acted as if rules and laws didn't apply to them. While it was true that the hospital was a tenant command with its own CO and administration, it was still part of the base and the United States Navy. But I'm not sure that we could convince some of the medical personnel.

My oldest son, Jim, was a volunteer at the base hospital. One morning as I was going to the office in the War Wagon, Jim asked me to drop him off at the hospital. We approached an intersection near the small boat marina that connected with the road that leads to the hilltop hospital. The intersection was always a bottleneck, so there were several cars at the stop sign waiting for the cross traffic to clear.

The driver of a car about two vehicles in front of us decided not to wait, so he cut across an expansive lawn, thereby going around the stop sign. I couldn't believe what I had just seen, so I turned on the emergency lights and siren, and gave chase. The driver, a doctor assigned to the hospital, pulled over, and stopped on the lawn. I gave him a citation for driving on the lawn in violation of road and driving rules. That kind of driving, in police circles, is known as misdemeanor stupid. I returned to the War Wagon, dropped Jim off at the hospital, and then went to the office.

When I got home that evening, Jim told me that I no longer had to drive him to work at the hospital. The doctors had gotten together and decided that it was in their best interest to form a carpool to pick up Jim each morning so that I wouldn't be in the area when they decided to break the road and driving rules, which apparently was often.

I agreed that the doctors could do the driving. Then I called the dispatcher and assigned a patrol unit to park at that same intersection each workday morning from 0730 to 0815 for the purpose of citing violations of road and driving rules.

When Jim got home the next night, he said, "Dad, you better not get sick while you are assigned to Roosevelt Roads. They really hate you over there. You might not survive the medical treatment."

He was exaggerating, of course, but I felt that there was some merit to what he had said. There was however, one Flight Surgeon who I trusted implicitly. I always went to see him when I needed medical attention. If the flight surgeon wasn't available, I waited until he was available. That's life as the town sheriff!

The hospital CO was a medical doctor who was somewhat renowned for having designed the naval station's modern medical facility some years earlier. He too was prone to pushing his weight around.

He was about an hour or so late arriving at a formal dinner for naval station officers at the O'Club. This was a time when there was a valid threat against the admiral who was also attending the dinner. The admiral was seated at the head table along with the naval station CO and XO and their wives.

NIS agents and I had agreed on a tactical placing of armed agents and myself to protect the admiral and the senior officers at the head table in the event that an assassination was attempted. The hospital CO, a Medical Corps captain, expected to be seated at the head table, but the Maître d' explained that he would have to get the approval of the security officer, who was an ensign. I said no to the request, indicating that the Medical Corps captain would have to be seated with the other officers. The captain left the club in a huff, without dinner. It wasn't personal.

Chapter 6.24 The Cliff House Incident

An incident that became the biggest brouhaha at the time was my request for a cliff house. A warrant officer moved out of Navy officer quarters located across the street from the captain's quarters. I wanted the house for two reasons.

1. It made sense to me that the Security Officer, who was responsible for the security of the CO and his family, would be better located across the street in the event that it became necessary to respond to an incident at the skipper's house.

2. There was a large lawn at the cliff house, which allowed me more space to erect an antenna for amateur radio operations.

I went to see Captain Keathley and explained that the house was vacant and that as a department head, the CO's security officer, and an amateur radio operator, I should be allowed to live in the cliff house. Captain Keathley said that he would get back to me. About a week later, he gave me permission to move into the house.

The brouhaha started when a lieutenant commander from one of the two admiral's staffs on the base decided he wanted the quarters. Since I was just a lieutenant, he believed that he should get the house. The captain disagreed. He had made his decision and he was going to stick by it. The admiral called and demanded that the house be assigned to the lieutenant commander. The captain refused. It was his base, and he would make the decision as to who would get what quarters.

The next call was from the office of the Chief of Naval Operations (CNO). They wanted to know why a more senior officer didn't get the house. The captain stuck by his guns. I don't know how much trouble that caused the captain, but any trouble is not good.

Months later, during a formal officer's dinner at the O'Club, the featured speaker, an admiral from a command in the states, suddenly died. Captain Keathley assigned the task of finding another speaker to the XO. Captain Smith grabbed a few junior officers, including me, and assigned us a topic on which we were to speak for three minutes. My topic was, "Why I Rate a Cliff House."

I started out my speech by saying, "while I fully recognize that most of you are much more rank than I..." The double meaning of the word "rank" finally hit the senior officers. They weren't impressed with my speech.

The Cliff House and my Little Red Truck (Photo by John Cline)

Chapter 6.25 The Fun for Lunch Bunch

Meals were a time to socialize. Formal dinners at the O'Club were interspersed with barbeques on Officer's Beach for officers and their families. Impromptu barbeques between friends and neighbors were commonplace when there was no war or other international incident that kept personnel working day and night. The Fun for Lunch Bunch evolved because many officers ate lunch at the O'Club at least a couple of times a week. Of course friends and co-workers ate together.

At one particular luncheon, I came up with the idea that to become a member of the "Fun for Lunch Bunch," the candidate had to eat a particularly grotesque dessert that started with a large strawberry sundae and a huge concoction of various forms of ice cream, fruits, and syrups. It was almost guaranteed to put another five pounds on the person eating it.

It was permissible however, for the candidate to share the concoction with the rest of the crowd, if sharing occurred to the candidate. Many didn't think of sharing and ate the whole thing.

Clint Smith, Rod Kelley, Dick MacCullagh, Jim Adkins, their wives, Pat, and others were all duly initiated members of the Fun for Lunch Bunch. Visitors from the States had heard of the initiation and wanted to become members. But of course they had to be invited by an already established member, and they had to be initiated. One of my favorite members was a fighter pilot from VC- 8 with the call sign "Peaches."

Peaches fit in with the Fun for Lunch Bunch very well. When she was in pilot training, she had an aircraft accident. The wreckage was said to have been so bad that it was a miracle that she survived. Because she was one of the Navy's first female fighter pilot trainees, her injuries might have affected whether other females would be allowed to fly fighters in the Navy.

She recovered, graduated, and took her place as a fighter jock at VC-8. Years later, she became the commanding officer of her own squadron.

Peaches added to the Fun for Lunch Bunch because she had an infectious laugh, and like her male naval aviator counterparts, she enjoyed a good prank.

Once when she was flying, I tuned to her squadron's tactical radio frequency and called "Peaches."

"Who's that?" she questioned. I would be one of the last people who she would expect to hear on the squadron's frequency.

"God," I said in my deepest voice. She didn't buy it.

Fighter Pilot - Call Sign "Peaches" (Photo by John Cline)

Peaches had said that she would join us at the O'Club for lunch if I would pick her up at the Administration building at noon. She was in one of those classes that military members must suffer through that has nothing to do with their jobs, but does have a lot to do with being a member of the military. I arrived on time, but the instructor kept droning on.

I went into the classroom and asked the instructor if the lieutenant was in the class. "Yes," he said.

"Would you point her out?" I asked.

He did. I went over and asked her to stand. I placed her in handcuffs and walked her out of the class. We went to lunch at the O'Club with the rest of the Fun for Lunch Bunch. I don't know why I didn't get in trouble for that stunt. She never did tell me what she went through when she returned to class for the afternoon session.

The Fun for Lunch Bunch was just that – fun!

Chapter 6.26 Dinner with Great Britain's Prince Andrew

A lot of senior military personnel and government officials came to Roosevelt Roads, especially during the winter months. For the most part, putting on the extra security required of a visitor's rank or position was boring but necessary. But this time, even I was impressed.

Even though I was responsible for the security on the base, I had no need to know what Roosevelt Roads was doing to support Great Britain in the war with Argentina over the Falkland Islands.

One of our tenant commands, Commander, South Atlantic Force, U.S. Atlantic Fleet, was headquartered at Roosy Roads when he wasn't at sea, and was closely allied with the navies of South American countries, including Argentina. In fact, since 1960, they had often participated in exercises called "UNITAS" with the navies of South and Central America. Conversely, our nation's long standing history with Great Britain dictated that we support them during the war. Because we also had a relationship with Argentina, support for Great Britain had to be somewhat covert.

Because I was out of the information loop, I have no idea how we may have supported Great Britain during the Falklands war. I do know that Secretary of State, Henry Kissinger, came to Roosy Roads once or twice while his airplane was refueled for his trip back to Washington. Otherwise, I got my information like everyone else, from the evening news on television.

In early July 1982, following the June 14, 1982 cessation of hostilities, I was called to the CO's office. Captain Keathley told me that a British ship was going to tie up to the Roosevelt Roads pier to refuel, and would remain overnight. Further, there would be a barbeque for the ship's officers to be hosted by the officers from Roosevelt Roads. My job was to provide security for Prince Andrew, who was part of the ship's crew. No one was to know that he was attending the barbeque. We were to use a false name that the prince commonly used when he was in public, but not acting in an official capacity.

That evening, I met with the prince and explained that I would be his security detail. He was to remain with me at all times, and if there was anything he needed, I would try to accommodate him.

I made arrangements as quietly as possible to seat the prince with Captain Jim Keathley and his wife Billie, Pat, and me at a table under the cabana at Officer's Beach. The other British officers were scattered among the rest of the American naval officers.

It was a typical Puerto Rican evening. The sun had set, the tiki torches were lit, most of the officers were wearing bathing suits and guayberas, and there was just a hint of coolness in the evening air. There was more than enough food and beer to go around.

We avoided talking about the war and the battles that the British seagoing warriors had just fought. Rather, the repartee was lighthearted. Captain Jim Keathley welcomed the British officers and we enjoyed our companionship together.

Some of the officers played horseshoes in pits near the cabana. Prince Andrew seemed to take an interest, so I asked if he would like to play. He indicated that he had never played horseshoes, so I explained the rules. We threw a few horseshoes. The prince said that throwing horseshoes was harder than he expected. I remarked that we were taking it easy on him since he was new to the game.

"How so?" he asked.

"Well usually we throw shoes with the horses still attached."

For a moment it looked as if he was trying to decipher my Americanized English – mentally translating what I had said. He looked at me with a surprised look and I had to admit that I was joking.

The British ship left at daybreak. The morning newspapers revealed that Britain's Prince Andrew had stopped by Roosevelt Roads along with the crew, and that the ship's officers had attended a barbeque hosted by the officers of Roosevelt Roads.

My wife read the article and asked, "Which one was the prince?"

Teasingly I answered, "Didn't you recognize him? You had dinner with him."

She was horrified. She had been casually talking with royalty and had no idea. She asked, "You couldn't tell your wife?"

Across the street, the same scene was playing out in the CO's quarters. Of course Captain Keathley had an out – he reportedly told Billie that "John wouldn't let me tell you," or words that effect.

Both Billie and Patsy have often proclaimed their displeasure at my silence. I just shrug and smile saying, "Security you know."

To this day, they are not amused. But Jim Keathley and I laugh at the retelling of the story.

Chapter 6.27 "That's My Airplane:" The Invasion of Grenada

In preparation for the invasion of Grenada, President Reagan made it clear that communications about the invasion would be passed only on a "need to know" basis. Nothing was to be passed by radio or telephone. Information would be passed in person, as needed. An Air Force general flew in to Roosy and briefed the admiral and Captain Keathley. Two Air Force Airborne Warning and Control System (AWACS) aircraft would be arriving in a few days to prepare for the invasion. I was briefed because the aircraft required a specific level of security as prescribed by the Air Force.

I knew that our Security Department didn't have sufficient personnel needed for the type of security that the Air Force required on the flight line while simultaneously performing other duties on the base.

There was some concern about the reaction of some Puerto Ricans as a result of the invasion. We had to plan for the possibility that the Macheteros, or some other group, might attack the base. We had to increase patrols in the undeveloped areas of the base. I suggested that we contact the Air Force and ask for a squad of Air Force Security Police to provide the required level of security for the AWACS aircraft. Captain Keathley agreed.

I called a former classmate from the Lackland security school who was assigned to the Air Force Security Police Operations Center. I told him only that we had some Air Force aircraft that needed level one protection and that I didn't have the personnel to do the job. He indicated that they could provide the personnel if we would send a message request to his command. I prepared the message and took it to the captain for release. The next morning, the CO called indicating that Second Fleet had sent a message indicating that we were not to use Air Force personnel, but rather that we would provide the needed security using "in house" assets.

Second Fleet was also Commander, Joint Task Force 120, meaning he was in charge of the invasion forces, so Captain Keathley had no option other than to obey the Second Fleet order.

Second Fleet had absolutely no knowledge of what resources we had, but he had made a command decision without talking with our CO. We were stuck with implementing that decision. The captain suggested that I contact the CO of the Marine Detachment to see if they would be willing to handle flightline security for the AWACS. Colonel Bill Vacca agreed. The detachment gunnery sergeant was briefed regarding Air Force security requirements for the AWACS, and the flightline security mission was passed to the Marine detachment.

In September 1983, the AWACS aircraft arrived. The pilots of the AWACS are colonels, what is popularly known as bird colonels, the equivalent of our naval station CO, and XO. The pilots were briefed on the fact that the Marines would be guarding their aircraft. They should have paid close attention to that statement. After flying the mission for the day, the aircraft were locked and custody of the aircraft was passed to the Marine sentries for the night.

The next morning, an Air Force master sergeant, one of the crewmen on the AWACS, walked from Air Operations to the flightline. As he approached one of the AWACS aircraft, the Marine sentry shouted, "Halt!"

The master sergeant waved and said "It's okay, I'm part of the crew."

The sentry again yelled, "Halt!"

And once again the master sergeant kept walking toward the aircraft. The Marine yelled halt a third time then hit the master sergeant in the stomach with the butt of his loaded M-16, ordering the master sergeant to lie down on the ground. The sergeant did as he was told. The Marine sentry called for the Sergeant of the Guard.

The morning sun was hot and the tarmac was broiling. The master sergeant lay on the tarmac with his fingers interlaced on the back of his head and his ankles crossed. As they were waiting for the Sergeant of the Guard, the pilot walked toward the aircraft from Air Operations, oblivious to his crewman lying on the tarmac.

As the colonel approached the aircraft, the Marine sentry yelled, "Halt!"

The colonel kept walking toward the aircraft. "Halt," the sentry yelled a second time.

The pilot, who was in his flight suit and who probably thought that his uniform was all he needed to approach the aircraft, kept walking.

Halt," the Marine shouted, following the order with a butt strike to the pilot's midsection. "Down on the ground now."

The colonel got down in the prone position, interlocking his fingers and crossing his ankles as ordered by the Marine sentry. It was about then that the Sergeant of the Guard arrived.

Seeing the colonel on the tarmac, he muttered, "This is above my pay grade," and called the Marine detachment (MARDET) office asking for the CO.

He did, however, allow the colonel and the master sergeant to stand up, thereby allowing them to remove their bodies from the hot tarmac.

Colonel Vacca arrived at the AWACS flightline.

The Air Force Colonel was highly pissed off and told the MARDET CO, "That's my aircraft."

Bill Vacca answered, "No sir, that aircraft is the property of the naval station security officer."

"What?" exclaimed the exasperated pilot.

Colonel Vacca said, "Air Force regulations require that you provide the Marine sentry with a crew list. Did you do that?"

"No," the pilot admitted.

"Well, now the aircraft belongs to the security officer until we can determine who the crew of the aircraft is."

That's when they called me.

When I arrived at the flightline, I called the Air Force colonel aside and asked, "You've never actually worked with Marines before, have you?"

"No," he admitted.

"Well, Colonel," I said, "they take everything literally. They were told not to allow anyone near the aircraft who wasn't on the crew list. But because you didn't give them a crew list, nobody gets near the AWACS aircraft. Do we understand how the system works now? I asked."

"Yes," he said.

Behind me, I heard another Marine sentry yell, Halt! Oh God, here we go again, I thought.

But Colonel Vacca put a stop to the rest of the process and each aircraft was eventually turned over to their respective air crew as they arrived on the flightline.

NOTE: A few weeks later, hours prior to the actual invasion, three AWACS aircraft landed and were positioned on the tarmac. The pilot of the lead aircraft exited the plane and was observed franticly waving and yelling, "Who wants my crew list? – Here's my crew list." They learn fast, these Air Force guys.

Chapter 6.28 Infiltration at the Back Gate

Colonel Vacca called just after three in the morning saying, "There's been an incident at the back gate. I'll pick you up in five minutes."

I hurriedly dressed in khakis, loaded and holstered my .45 and met Bill for the ride to the back gate.

"What's going on?" I asked.

"I don't know for sure, but there was report of an infiltration at the back gate. Shots were fired," he said.

Colonel Bill Vacca, CO Marine Detachment (Photo by John Cline)

We rode in silence the few miles to the back gate. When we arrived, the Sergeant of the Guard was chewing out the Marine sentry. Bill parked his vehicle and we walked to the gate where a dead cow was laying in the middle of the incoming lane.

"What happened?" the colonel asked.

The Sergeant of the Guard answered, "This sentry shot the cow."

The Colonel shifted his gaze to the sentry and asked, "Why?" "Didn't have an ID card, sir," the sentry answered.

I walked back to Bill's truck. This was clearly a Marine CO matter, not a security officer problem. I caught a ride to my quarters with a police officer. I don't know if Bill got back to his quarters that night, but the naval station had to pay the farmer a rather exorbitant price for the dead cow.

Chapter 6.29 Talking to Grenada by Ham Radio

Clint Smith and I were having lunch at the O'Club a couple of days before the invasion of Grenada. I was telling Clint how amateur radio operators could link island repeaters so that hams could talk to the various islands. He asked whether we could talk to someone on Grenada.

"Sure," I said, as I took my handheld two meter Ham Radio out and punched up the required tone code.

I called CQ and a radio amateur on Grenada with whom I had talked on several occasions answered immediately. After the usual greetings, he asked, "Hey, John, when are you guys going to start the invasion?"

I was shocked that he would ask that question over the radio. I couldn't answer him, so I broke the connection and turned off the radio. Clint and I just looked at each other silently. The coming invasion was obviously no secret.

Chapter 6.30 Orders from the White House

The invasion began early in the morning hours of October 25, 1983. Meanwhile, we were supporting the invasion with a runway and logistical supplies. We had no direct role in the combat. I was running around the base in the War Wagon when I got a radio call from the police dispatcher who said, "You better get home fast. Your wife called and there's some kind of emergency."

Once again, my heart started pounding as I pointed the War Wagon toward my quarters. When I arrived, Pat said, "You have a priority call from Fort Buchanan on the radio."

Well first, I was surprised that I had left the high frequency radio on. Secondly, I was surprised to get a call from a radio operator at Fort Buchanan who could have just as easily called me on the phone.

I pushed the mic button and said, "Calling station, this is NN0IPJ, over."

The San Juan Army radio operator came back immediately, identifying his station call sign and saying, "I have a priority message for you."

"Send your message," I said. He said, "message follows:

PRIORITY, TIME 270600Z OCT 1983 FROM: THE WHITE HOUSE

TO: LIEUTENANT JOHN CLINE, NAVAL STATION ROOSEVELT ROADS, P.R.

SUBJECT: GRENADA BT

YOU ARE DIRECTED TO MEET MILITARY FLIGHT AND INSTALL NEW REPEATER ON GRENADA TO RESTORE RADIO COMMUNICATIONS WITH OFFICIALS FROM OTHER ISLAND NATIONS.

BT"

What? Who gets orders from the White House by way of the Military Affiliate Radio System (MARS), the military's version of ham radio? I asked the Army radio operator to stand by and told him that he would need to repeat the message as soon as I could get the CO and XO to the radio.

I called the CO and XO by phone and asked them to come to my quarters at once. They did, first the CO who lived across the street, and then the XO who lived on the other end of officer housing.

They were ushered into the bedroom where the radio station was set up, along with two large teletype machines.

The XO, the same prank-loving Clint Smith of "Dinner with the XO story," pointed at our bed and started singing, "You didn't make your bed, – You didn't make your bed." Patsy was mortified. Our bed has been made every day since.

After hearing the radio message, Captain Keathley turned and asked me, "What are you going to do?"

I said, "Well, I'm not going to say no to the President of United States, but I will ask them to send a copy of the orders to AIRLANT (Commander, Atlantic Fleet)."

Clint Smith smiled and said, "Oh John, you're just trying to get another medal."

Nothing could have been farther from the truth. I composed and sent a message back to the White House through the San Juan Army MARS radio operator. My message said that I would carry out the orders, but I also requested that a copy of the orders be sent to AIRLANT. I never heard another word about the mission. I learned months later that the mission had been reassigned to the Army.

Chapter 6.31 Intelligence Gathering by Ham Radio

U.S. Army Rangers had safely removed American students from the True Blue campus at St George's Medical Center on Grenada. However, Cuban soldiers and soldiers of the People's Revolutionary Army (PRA), who were retreating, blocked the Rangers from an early rescue of American students at the Grand Anse campus. Military planners evidently didn't realize that the American students were scattered over three different campuses.

Other objectives, such as the removal of the People's Revolutionary Government and restoration of the lawful government were starting to bog down. Neutralizing resistance turned out to be more difficult than expected in some areas. American military personnel from all services found that radio communication was not well coordinated. In fact, American forces didn't even have island topographical maps, so it was difficult for them to determine where the enemy's command center and logistical sites were located. Military objectives were bogging down due mainly to poor intelligence.

Grenadian citizens, those who had left the island before the invasion began, contacted ham radio operators in other island nations throughout the Caribbean. They provided specific information about the location of weapons storage sites, communications centers, and the command center at Fort Frederick, which wasn't on any maps. U.S. military planners didn't know of the existence of Fort Frederick, the nerve center for Cuban and PRA troops. Grenadians knew exactly where those enemy military resources were located because they had been forced to build them. But what was a Ham Radio Operator supposed to do with that information, and who would they pass it to?

The first radio call came in on the evening of the second night following the initial phase of the invasion. I had checked into the Caribbean Island Net, a high frequency radio net that tied all of the island nations together by Ham Radio for the purpose of passing message traffic and weather conditions. This network was especially vital during hurricane season. I was surprised when the Net Control Station said, "I have three messages for you from multiple locations."

I took the calling stations off to another frequency and started copying down the information.

It quickly became apparent that the information that they were providing was "intelligence" that would be valuable to our forces on Grenada.

As soon as I received the three messages, I passed the information to the intelligence officer at the headquarters of the Commander, Naval Forces, Caribbean. He put the data into a naval message and sent it to the Intelligence Officer at Second Fleet. The message was received at Second Fleet in less than thirty minutes. More information came in by amateur radio on the following evening. Once again, I called the intel officer at COMNAVFORCARIB. Once again the information was quickly forwarded to Second Fleet.

On the morning of October 28th, I received a telephone call from the office of the Chief of Naval Operations. The commander on the other end of the line told me that the information that I was receiving from hams all over the Caribbean was more important than my job as security officer, and that I was to monitor the ham radio frequencies until further notice. Most of the information that I received came in on October 26, 27, and 28. The few messages that I received after that didn't add a lot to what had already been received.

Few people, even today, know that amateur radio played an intelligence-gathering role during the invasion of Grenada. Neither the radio amateurs nor the Grenadian citizens who provided the information received recognition for their efforts. They saved lives (on both sides) and significantly contributed to bringing hostilities to a timely end.

In all, the fighting lasted about a week. Once the Fort Frederick command center was destroyed, resistance quickly died down. According to an unclassified report, U.S. military personnel were confronted by 1200 PRA soldiers, 780 Cubans, 49 Soviets, 24 North Koreans, 16 East Germans, 14 Bulgarians, and a few Libyans. Nearly 600 Americans and 80 foreign nationals were safely evacuated.

Amateur radio station when I was on active duty (Photo by John Cline)

American and Cuban wounded were sent to the naval hospital at Roosevelt Roads. Army military police from Fort Buchanan provided protection for Cubans who were sent to a San Juan hospital with head injuries. The wounded were eventually returned to Cuba under the auspices of the International Red Cross.

Chapter 6.32 Ocean Venture 84

The most improbable set of circumstances occurred on the evening of April 25, 1984. The phone in my quarters rang just as we were sitting down to dinner. Merissa, the admiral's secretary, said, "The admiral would like to see you in his office right away."

I thanked her and shifted from civilian clothes into my khaki uniform and drove to the admiral's office. He wasn't there. Neither was anyone else, including Merissa.

The building was mostly dark; the only light was sunlight coming through the windows in the outer offices that lined the passageways. I walked through the passageways looking in each office until I heard voices emanating from the conference room. I opened one of the double doors and saw the admiral talking to a room packed with commanders, captains, and a few civilians. There were about thirty people in all.

I entered the room as quietly as possible, intending to stand in the back until the admiral was ready to talk with me. Then I heard him say the words, "I am placing LTJG Cline in charge of security operations for Ocean Venture 84." Everyone suddenly shifted their gaze to me.

I had no idea what the admiral was talking about. The only thing I was in charge of was base security. Ocean Venture was a really big deal involving ships, and embarked Marines, who would storm the beaches of Vieques with men and equipment to exercise and test invasion readiness. How could I be in charge of something to do with that? Then he said something that put absolute fear into my heart.

He said, "It's your meeting, John."

My meeting? I didn't even know why I was there. I walked to the front of the room where the admiral handed me a sheet of paper outlining my orders. The order read:

"1. You are hereby designated as the Officer in Charge of special law enforcement/security operations for OCEAN VENTURE 84. You shall coordinate the on-scene efforts of Navy, Coast Guard, and U.S. Marshal Units assigned for the purposes of enforcing regulations pertaining to trespass in the Vieques danger and restricted areas."

About thirty pairs of eyes were on me, and not one set of them was friendly. Senior officers including captains of ships and special agents from various law enforcement agencies are not prone to taking orders from a lieutenant junior grade.

The purpose of Ocean Venture 84 was to enhance the U.S. capability to project military power in support of friendly nations in the Caribbean. The exercise was designed to test the rapid deployment capability of military units. It involved over 30,000 military personnel from units including the 82nd Airborne, the 26th Marine Amphibious Unit, and 250 Strategic Air Command and Tactical Command aircraft. The exercise area included the entire eastern coast of the United States, the Straits of Florida, and the Caribbean to the Gulf of Mexico.

Much of the exercise had started five days earlier. Our part in Ocean Venture 84 was to take place in a couple of days, and would include an amphibious landing and air assaults on Vieques.

My job was to ensure nothing interfered with the ships, landing craft, and personnel. Once again, the threat of terrorism was a concern.

I have no idea what I said to that group of senior officers and agents. I remember circulating a contact sheet so that I would have the names, agencies, and telephone numbers of the people in the room. I remember asking if they had any questions about the mission. But the meeting was a blur. No questions were asked, and the meeting concluded. I looked for the admiral to refine the written orders, but he had already left the building. Once again, I was on my own.

The next morning, I met with the Security Department's division chiefs, including the Patrol, Military Working Dog, and WASP Boat Divisions. We started planning for the security of the three ships and the amphibious landing that would take place during our part in the exercise. We anticipated that intruders would likely come from land and sea, so we had to plan for any eventuality.

Before the amphibious landing could take place, a fly over of the danger zone confirmed there was no one in the restricted area. Very often, people form Vieques entered the restricted areas to remove brass from expended ordnance. This was dangerous because there was always the possibility that some of the ordnance had not exploded. Also, live ammunition would be used prior to the amphibious landing, so we had to ensure that no unauthorized civilians would be killed or injured as a result of the exercise. We had three aircraft, one fixed wing C-12 and two helicopters providing airborne range patrol and an overhead observation platform.

To ensure that the three ships were not attacked, or that intruders did not interfere with the amphibious landing, we had ten patrol boats, which included Coast Guard boats, our two WASP boats, and a Coast Guard Cutter. Security personnel were comprised of the men and women of the Roosy Roads security department. We also had members of the U.S. Marshal's office on- scene.

The Atlantic Fleet Weapons Training Facility had a tower that overlooked the impact range, but not the amphibious landing zone. The tower had a radio communications package that could talk with all of the ships, law enforcement agencies, and commercial aviation. Commercial aircraft were not allowed to fly over restricted areas when the range was in use. The downside was that I could not see the ships or the amphibious landing area. I would have to rely on security and law enforcement personnel to keep me informed of what was happening on the beaches where the amphibious landing was to take place.

The three U.S. Navy ships with their embarked Marines pulled up to their designated positions, which I had chosen simply by looking at a map with grid squares. The WASP boat senior chief called me on the radio and said that the ships were too close together. I repositioned the ships placing them within two grid squares of each other.

They would need the additional space to run boats for the amphibious landing. The senior chief probably saved me from an embarrassing situation. Thanks, senior chief!

The exercise went relatively well. One man in a really fast boat attempted to enter the restricted zone but was herded out of the area by the WASP boats. About an hour later, he returned and actually got inside the restricted area.

The WASP boats stopped him with some magnificent maneuvering and placed him in handcuffs. They were about to pass him off to the Coast Guard when the man pleaded for another chance. Once you place a suspect in handcuffs, it's pretty well understood that the person is under arrest. However, there are times when the police can call the restraint a detention rather than an arrest. I chose to do that in this case because the intruder clearly was a protester, not a terrorist. The intruder was released and was told not to return. He didn't. But he went to town telling everyone that he had penetrated the restricted zone in defiance of the Navy.

Good security can be boring. If you prevent an attack, you keep looking for things that don't occur. Such was the case during the exercise. While the exercise was still on-going, the captain of the Coast Guard cutter suddenly told me that he was leaving for St. Thomas even though the exercise was not concluded. I needed the cutter to stay on station in case we did have a terrorist attack or even a sizable protest. The Coast Guard captain and I had a very strained conversation, after which the he agreed to stay on station until the exercise concluded a few hours later.

A few days following the conclusion of the exercise, I received a call from the admiral. He was angry.

"Why haven't you charged the intruder?" he asked. "Because we only detained the suspect," I answered.

The admiral wanted me to file charges. The intruder was still mocking the Navy in town and the admiral did not like having the Navy mocked.

The admiral slammed the phone down into the cradle. The crash of the phone was the last sound that I heard about the security we provided for Ocean Venture 84.

So why didn't I arrest him? Because I had to consider that he was merely a distraction, a decoy; that while we were using resources to arrest him, tow his boat to shore, fill out all the paperwork, and take him to a federal lockup in San Juan, a larger and more aggressive flotilla would attempt to disrupt the exercise. I kept looking for the threat. And one man sticking his middle finger at the Navy was not a threat that would disrupt the exercise. We could have filed charges even at that late date, but the admiral never gave me an order, so I chose to let the matter die.

Chapter 6.33 "I'm Pregnant and it's all John's fault." (April 1984)

In early March 1984, the Assistant Security Officer, a warrant officer named Wayne, and I gave a set of handcuffs bedecked with stars and glitter to BJ (Gary Bjorklund). I don't remember why.

During a naval station officer's barbeque at Officer's Beach in late April 84, Captain Keathley had just finished giving the officers a "well done" speech. As was his custom, he asked if anyone had any comments. BJ's wife, Dorothy, stood and when recognized by Captain Keathley, stated in a loud voice, "I'm pregnant and it's all John's fault."

The sudden silence was deafening. All eyes, including my wife's, shifted to me. Then all eyes focused on BJ. Everyone expected him to punch me out, or worse.

Instead, he smiled and said, "No, it's not John's child, but he was most definitely the cause."

Evidently, the handcuffs had led to an amorous evening.

Nine months later, while I was at the FBI National Academy, I received an arrival notice in the mail. James Robert Bjorklund (alias John Wayne) was born at 10:28 a.m. on January 6th, 1985. I wonder if he was ever told why we call him John Wayne.

Chapter 6.34 Talking With Santa

My favorite use of amateur radio is setting up a station at hospitals or shopping centers and letting kids talk with Santa at the North Pole.

I got permission from the Navy Exchange Officer to set up a station in front of the store on a weekend about two weeks before Christmas. One by one the kids came up to the radio operator, who helped the children talk to Santa by radio.

What really made the radio call magic was that Santa seemed to know everything about every caller, child or adult. As Santa talked with the children, he called each child by name without seemingly being told the name of the child. He knew the names of the caller's best friends, pets, favorite foods, television shows, toys, and teachers.

That magic was made possible by helpers who talked with parents in the background, then passed the personal information by radio on a separate frequency, to Santa at Santa's Village. The whole experience brought smiles to the faces of every child.

BJ brought his kids to talk with Santa. The kids had a delightful time and left believing that they had conversed with the real, the one and only, the true Santa Claus at the North Pole. The children were happy, the parents were happy, and Christmas was made just a little more special because of the experience.

A few months after Christmas, the Bjorklunds returned to civilian life. BJ returned to his former job flying for United Airlines. The family set up residence in Colorado. As the next Christmas approached, I received a call from BJ who started the conversation with, "John, we have a problem."

Apparently his kids wanted to talk with the real Santa. But they knew that could only happen through the magic of radio. I checked a directory and found a ham radio operator in their town. I called him and asked if he would be willing to run a phone patch for Gary's kids. He agreed, so once again the kids got to talk with Santa at the North Pole. Ham Radio is magic!

Chapter 6. 35 Visiting the Virgin Islands

Pat accepted an invitation for us to go to St. Thomas in the Virgin Islands for a weekend with Clint and Sue Smith. We took a side trip to a small island named St. John, also in the Virgin Islands. Two thirds of the island is a National Park.

The Park Service and its volunteers had placed cement placards underwater telling the snorkeling visitor what kind of fish and marine life were in the area. It was a truly wonderful experience.

Returning to Roosevelt Roads by boat from St. Thomas, I casually mentioned that I had really enjoyed myself, and that I was sorry that we had not made the trip sooner. Patsy had tried repeatedly over the past couple of years to get me to go. When she heard what I said, she responded by trying to throw me overboard. Oh, the ire of the woman!

The Beach at St John, U.S. Virgin Islands (Photo by John Cline)

Chapter 6.36 The Caribbean Police School

It is quite possible that the most important thing I ever did in my life was to get involved with the Caribbean Police School. That led to training the El Salvadorian "Special Investigative Unit" which was responsible for investigating death squads and human rights abuse cases in El Salvador.

In late 1984, FBI Special Agent David J. Kriskovich, known to everyone as Kris, came into the office to ask for the use of a classroom so that he could teach classes for the Caribbean Police School. Kris was on loan to the U.S. State Department which, with the FBI, had developed a curriculum for English-speaking Caribbean Basin police officers. The purpose of the classes was to teach police officers how to respond and investigate crimes effectively without becoming tyrannical.

Kris was a former Green Beret with distinctive service in Viet Nam. After serving in the Army for nine years, he joined the FBI in 1970. Besides the normal cases that a new FBI agent was typically assigned to, he also investigated terrorism, which few new agents got the chance to do.

Using his military and bureau experience, Kris developed the Special Weapons and Tactics (SWAT) concept and was one of the designers of the dreaded obstacle course at the FBI Academy at Quantico. In fact, he built a miniature obstacle course on his farm as a "confidence course" for his kids.

More importantly, he was the founder, developer, and director of the FBI's International Criminal Investigative Training Assistance Program (ICITAP), which came out of his experience with the Caribbean Police School, and from training the members of El Salvador's Special Investigative Unit (SIU). Kris was one of the most impressive human beings I have ever met. He was tall, good looking, and had an easy-going persona. Kris was an extremely likeable guy, and an effective Special Agent.

I didn't know it when he came into the office, but he had already run a couple of Caribbean Police School classes at Roosy. He had to beg and borrow whatever he could on the base to run his school. I became upset that no one had told me about the classes or the Caribbean Police School. And I was really upset that some other department head was the designated point of contact with Kris and the Caribbean Police School when it was so obvious that the school was a police matter and should have been assigned to me as the senior military police officer on the base.

I went to see Captain Keathley and aired my grievance. He immediately designated me as the point of contact for the FBI. I went into high gear to get the things that Kris would need, including a building that was remodeled for use as both the Security Department Training Unit and the Caribbean Police School. Then the Caribbean Police School had a real home.

By 1984, interior remodeling, using mainly volunteer labor, was completed and the fifth and sixth sessions of the Caribbean Police School were held. Then things got really difficult.

The U.S. State Department received a request from President Duarte of El Salvador to train military police personnel, who would become the nucleus of the SIU, which was formed to investigate death squads and human rights abuse cases.

Training Unit and Caribbean Police School (Photo by John Cline)

Kris was already on loan to State, and he was already training police personnel through the Caribbean Police School, so it was to him that the Department of State turned to get the job done. And that was no small job.

The State Department sponsored the training program for the El Salvadorian Military Police, the FBI would do the training, and the naval station would transport and house personnel, and provide training facilities. Since the El Salvadorians didn't speak English, it was necessary to have a translator for each group of four students. There were about twenty students in the class.

The FBI conducted background investigations on each student-candidate. Most of the experienced police officer candidates were not selected because investigation revealed that they had been corrupted or compromised by the criminal element or by politics. Twenty military police officers finally made it through the vetting process, but none of them had police experience. They had spent their first two years fighting rebels in the jungles and had not yet been assigned to law enforcement functions in the cities. So it became necessary to hold two separate courses: one for basic police work, and another for homicide investigations.

Almost everybody knew who was in charge of the death squads. Proving it was something else. Members of the SIU would be in constant danger. The people who ran the death squads were powerful and well-connected. Killing a military policeman and his family would mean nothing to them.

The SIU Commanding Officer was basically a figurehead. The real authority had been placed with the Executive Officer. His life expectancy, when he returned to El Salvador, was fifteen seconds. His wife was so afraid that she took the children and left him. Yet the XO, who was devoted to President Duarte, was up to the task, and remained resolute.

We did what we could to make the students feel at home. But it was tough on them. For nearly two years they had been fighting rebels, and now they were in a crowded classroom trying to learn how to become police officers in a civil environment. They were learning investigative techniques that might get them killed. Of the twenty students selected for the first class, only one had to be returned to El Salvador for unsatisfactory behavior. The rest of the students were committed, but they fully realized the dangers to which they would be returning.

After training, the students returned to El Salvador where they became members of the SIU. Gary Bjorklund flew the SIU executive officer back to San Salvador, and reported that no one wanted to stand next to the XO when they arrived. Just about everyone thought he would be killed at the airport. He wasn't.

David Kriskovich at the SIU Graduation Banquet (Photo by John Cline)

A few years later, Kris told me that President Duarte had been diagnosed with cancer. Before the president died, he told Kris that the SIU had saved the lives of over 5,000 people each year. That's how many people were not killed by death squads when compared with recent years gone by. Kris presented me with a gift from President Duarte, a machete bearing the presidential seal. Working with Kris and formulating the SIU was probably the most important thing I have ever done in my lifetime in terms of saving lives.

Kris had arranged for me to get an invitation to attend the FBI National Academy in 1984, but the captain wouldn't let me go for the three months that it would take to attend classes. Another opportunity occurred when I made the transition from Roosevelt Roads to my next duty station at Naval Submarine Base, San Diego (SUBASE).

Kris arranged an invitation for me to attend classes starting in January 1985. However, the security officer detailer refused to allow it. He wanted me to report to the SUBASE early in January.

Kris called the director of the FBI, who called the Chief of Naval Operations, who called the Chief of Naval Personnel, who called the detailer saying that I was to be authorized to attend the FBI National Academy. But the detailer got the last laugh. I had to attend the academy at my own cost. The Navy would not pay any expenses.

I was not the first Navy man to attend the FBI National Academy. I think that honor fell to Don Romeo, who was one of the warrant officers with whom I attended the schools at Lackland Air Force Base. He went to the FBINA when he was a chief petty officer. But I believe that I was the first naval officer to attend.

Captain Frank Mezzadri (of Blue Angels fame) and who had relieved Captain Keathley as Commanding Officer of Naval Station Roosevelt Roads, allowed Patsy and the boys to remain at Roosy Roads until I graduated from the FBI National Academy. They would meet me in San Diego.

Note: For those who knew Frank, Captain Mezzadri died on the 28th of March, 2002, and he was buried in Arlington National Cemetery.

Captain Jim and Billie Keathley (Photos by John Cline)

Captain Clint and Sue Smith

Chaplain Rod and Trish Kelley (Photos by John Cline)

Senior Chaplain Dick & Marsha MacCullagh and son

Gary (BJ) & Dorothy Bjorklund and kids at their home in Colorado
- Gary is holding John Wayne (Photo by John Cline)

Captain Clint Smith, XO

Captain and Mrs. Mezzadri
(Photos by John Cline)

CHAPTER SEVEN

Chapter 7.1 The FBI National Academy

I left Roosevelt Roads and flew to Miami, Florida where I spent a wonderful New Year's Day with Billie and Jim Keathley, who had recently retired from naval service. I picked up my car, a 1970 Dodge Challenger, from Navy shipping. The battery was dead, gas had been drained from the tank to reduce the fire hazard while the vehicle was being shipped, and it was absolutely filthy. Stevedores jump-started the battery and poured a gallon of gas in the tank so that I could drive to the nearest gas station. I filled her up with gas, got a much needed car wash, and was off to Quantico, Virginia. I had to be there in two days, specifically between one and three in the afternoon.

In today's vernacular, the Challenger was a "muscle car." The body was free of dents and scratches, the drive train was in great shape, and it was a joy to drive. It had been a well-kept one-owner car when I bought it. And since it was a new car in Puerto Rico, it didn't have many of the things that we expect in cars nowadays. First, it didn't have electric windows. The seat belt was the old lap type. Most importantly, IT DIDN'T HAVE A HEATER.

The temperature got colder and colder as I drove north. The only warm clothes that I had were my dress blue uniform and a Navy Peacoat, which really wasn't all that warm after a couple of hours. Being a muscle car, the Challenger used a lot of gas.

At one point, I had to stop at a rural (one pump) gas station in South Carolina. Seemingly, it was in the middle of nowhere. The owner, dressed in dirty bib overalls, came out to fill the tank. He kept looking at my uniform and the license plate on the Challenger.

He said, "You don't look like no Puerto Rican (saying Rican as in Rick-in).

I explained that I had been stationed in Puerto Rico for the last three years, and was on my way to a new duty station.

He spat a chaw of tobacco and said, "Well, I guess that's okay."

It was a real "Deliverance" moment (reminiscent of the movie "Deliverance.")

The temperature continued to drop as I drove north. The only time I stopped was for gas, food, and to use the restroom. As night approached, I was so tired and so cold that I had to stop at a hotel. I registered as quickly as I could; my hand didn't function very well when I went to sign the registration card.

I went to my room where the first thing I did was to draw a tub full of hot water. I undressed, dropping my clothes on the floor and got in the tub where I stayed for at least a half hour, maybe more, until my body warmed. That was as close as I ever want to get to hypothermia. Early the next morning, I was up and, following a breakfast of black coffee, headed north again. The temperature continued to drop and there was snow all the way in to Quantico and the FBI Academy. In fact, according to the radio station weather jock, it was the coldest winter they had on record in over thirty-five years.

According to the written instructions, I was to have a sweat suit, gym trunks, and gym shoes. I had none of the above. I stopped at a K-Mart and picked up the required items. Although they didn't have sweat suits in my size, I got what I could, and continued on to the Academy, arriving within the required timeframe. I registered, got my room assignment, carried my gear to the room, and met my roomie, the Chief of Police of Solon, Ohio, Bob Bruckner.

In the eleven weeks that I shared a room with Bob, I learned that he was an outstanding police administrator and SWAT officer. And he was fastidious!

No matter how busy we got, no matter how pressed for time we were, his desk and living area were as neat as a pin. I, on the other hand, had a desk that looked like it had been arranged by a hand grenade.

In January 1985, I could not afford a laptop computer. Yet we had to type our assignments, especially our final papers. How it came to be, I don't know, but the instructors designated me to be the mentor for a Japanese student and a Swiss student, neither of whom spoke English very well. I spoke only a few words of Japanese and no French. Yet I was expected to help the two students with their papers. That's my only defense—but my desk really did look like it had been fragged. In fact the messy desk was so bad that Bob purchased a sign that reads, "A clean desk is a sign of a sick mind." I still have it.

After we checked in and stowed our gear, we went to the auditorium where members of the staff welcomed us. The Physical Fitness Director, Al Boccaccio, ended the session by telling us in glowing terms that we would now have the opportunity to tour the campus. He directed us to get into our running gear and to assemble in front of the gym. The running tour was only a few miles.

The snow was piled up along the walkways. The running paths were mostly free of snow. But it was cold. And for a guy who had spent the last three years in the tropics, it felt bitterly cold.

To make matters worse, the sweat suit that I bought was way too small, offering next to no protection from the elements. The trousers were about six inches too short, exposing my ankles. The top was tight across my chest. The material was thin and offered little warmth. To others, I must have looked very much the odd fellow. I got new sweats at the Marine Corps Exchange the next day.

Chapter 7.2 Constitutional Law Class

On the following day, our first class was Constitutional Law. There were two instructors, both Special Agents of the FBI and both lawyers. Thanks to Lieutenant Stornie of the Pasadena Police Department, my instructor at the Pasadena Police Academy and at Pasadena City College, I had a fairly solid background in Constitutional Law.

I admit that I enjoy collegial debate. Therefore, when questions of law come up, I'm usually right in the thick of the discussion. However, since I didn't want to get a reputation as the class loudmouth, I held back until it was clear that no one wanted to answer the question. I correctly answered several questions, some of which required the presentation of a brief review of the circumstances surrounding the case and the various trials that had resulted prior to the decision by the U.S. Supreme Court. I was able to provide both the decision of the Supreme Court and the review of the various cases, which prompted one of the instructors to approach me during a break asking if I was a lawyer. I assured her that I wasn't. Then she asked me to refrain from answering any more questions. So much for good intentions!

Most of the classes were a blur. When I first got to the National Academy, eleven weeks seemed like a lifetime. But as the work piled up, there suddenly wasn't enough time to do all of the research and writing necessary to get through all of the classes.

Chapter 7.3 Introduction to Terrorism

My favorite instructor and class was Introduction to Terrorism, taught by Special Agent Joe Conley. He was one of those extraordinarily dedicated types who went well out of his way to ensure that the student got all the information that he wanted and needed.

He was exceptionally well-versed in Middle Eastern terrorism and had a solid grasp on the history of terrorism. Unlike the lawyer in my Constitutional Law class, Joe encouraged me to talk about my experiences in Puerto Rico with the Macheteros and the FBI Counterterrorism Task Force. I didn't need a lot of encouragement. That was a time when people didn't rate terrorism high on the law enforcement priority list.

I chose "Terrorism in Puerto Rico" for my term paper because I thought that I could breeze through it. There wasn't a lot of information on terrorism in the FBI Academy's library. The library did contain an extensive amount of research material dealing with law enforcement. I'll bet the library is full of terrorism-related books now.

Like most academics, Joe had access to the libraries at a number of colleges and universities in the Virginia and Maryland areas. When I told him that there wasn't much in the way of research material on terrorism in Puerto Rico, he ordered books from other universities, sometimes spending his off duty hours personally driving to the campuses to pick up books and other research materials for my paper. In my opinion, that's the difference between a teacher and an instructor. Joe was a teacher.

My final paper wasn't as good as it should have been, or even as good as I would have liked it to be. I got so far behind helping the foreign students that my paper suffered. Joe wasn't the reader or the grader. That responsibility fell to another agent. I received a B, and after reading it years later thought that maybe I should have received a C. The information was good, but there were a lot of typographical errors that should have been corrected before I turned in the paper. I just ran out of time.

Chapter 7. 4 This Won't Hurt...

Astonishingly enough, the other class that I enjoyed most was physical fitness. Not because of the "no pain – no gain" philosophy, but because of Al Beccaccio. He looked like Mr. Atlas (the Arnold Schwarzenegger of his time) but he moved like a professional dancer, and was as suave as Gregory Peck. And he was smart. During one particular session, Al was teaching control holds. As we practiced controlling each other, I failed to properly initiate the control hold and my classmate easily got away. Al saw this and came over to me to demonstrate the proper way to implement the control hold. He whispered in my ear, "This won't hurt"—then after he had me well under control, he finished his sentence by saying "much" as the pain hit me. I hurt for the rest of the day.

Al and Kris Kriskovich were buddies. They had purchased forty acres in Spotsylvania, split the acreage into two parcels, and for many years were neighbors as well as close associates.

In between his classes in the Caribbean, Kris returned to the FBI Academy and took the time to check up on me to see how I was doing. He invited my roommate and me to meet his family. We went to dinner at the famous Mudd House, home of Dr. Samuel Mudd, who was convicted of complicity in the Lincoln assassination. Unknown to us at the time, it would be our last evening together.

Chapter 7.5 Bureaucracy Versus Common Sense

After about a week of attending classes, I started getting telephone calls from Captain Mezzadri in Puerto Rico regarding various new security-related problems at the naval station. He wanted to know if I would be willing to return to Roosy for another tour. As good as Roosy was for me, three years were enough. Another tour at Roosy didn't fit into my future plans. I was also getting calls from the Security Officer at Naval Submarine Base, San Diego who wanted me to leave the National Academy and to relieve him so that we would have a contact relief. No, I wouldn't leave the National Academy. Meanwhile, the cost of returning all those calls was adding up.

The FBI Academy is located on a Marine Corps base. They had autovon telephone lines, a telephone system specifically designed and paid for by the Department of Defense. I asked to use the autovon line and was refused permission. The clerk said that I would need the written permission of the FBI to use the autovon lines. I asked my class advisor who said he would check into it. The answer came back; no, students were not authorized to use the autovon lines. He had not heard the end of that issue.

At lunch the following day, Kris stopped by my table to say that the director wanted to see me at 1:00 p.m., and that I should invite my class advisor. The class advisor, a Special Agent of the FBI, took it for granted that the meeting was to be about the use of the autovon lines. I didn't tell him differently. He gave me that look that says, you worm, you're making life difficult for me. I just smiled.

We arrived at the director's office a few minutes early and were asked to wait until the director was available. My class advisor became more and more agitated. Finally, we were invited into the director's office where I was presented with a plaque from the FBI office in San Juan. Kris and the director beamed, and my class advisor appeared to look somewhat relieved. When the ceremony was concluded, the director said something to the effect of, if you need anything while you are at the Academy, just let me know. Of course I then said, well I could use access to the autovon phone line to conduct military business.

The director said, "No problem." He then looked at my class advisor and said, "Make sure he has access to the autovon lines."

Of course the class advisor answered, "Yes, sir."

Left to right: Class Advisor, John, and Kris
(FBI Academy Photo)

NOTE: Drawing on his experience managing the Caribbean Police School and administering the training of the El Salvadorian Special Investigative Unit, Special Agent **David Kriskovich** went on to train law enforcement officers globally through the International Criminal Investigative Training Assistance Program that he helped form, and later after his retirement from the bureau, as the Deputy Director of the International Police Task Force in Bosnia.

> **He and Livio (Al) Beccaccio** died in central Bosnia on September 17, 1997 when the United Nations helicopter they were riding in crashed into a mountainside as a result of dense fog.

Chapter 7.6 All the Seafood You Can Eat

Meals at the academy were catered. They had a kitchen, and the meals were cooked on site. But the kitchen crew was under contract.

The food was generally very good. A little over halfway through our stay at the academy, the Food Service Manager decided to have an "all you can eat" seafood night. He made a strategic error when he said "all you can eat." My roommate and I went to dinner not knowing until we got to the dining room that the menu was seafood or that we could eat our fill.

Bob liked the Alaskan crab legs. I liked the shrimp, although I would have preferred lobster. They didn't have lobster on the menu. We started eating with no particular goal in mind. People came and went and we just continued to eat and talk. I sat across from Bob, who placed the empty crab leg shells on a platter in front of him. I placed the boiled shrimp peelings in bowls next to me on the table. We kept eating and talking until I suddenly realized that I couldn't see Bob any more. The pile of crab leg shells was so tall that although I was sitting directly across from Bob, I couldn't see him.

As we were leaving, the Food Service Manager came up to me and said, "I hope you're satisfied. We will never again have an all- you-can-eat seafood night."

I never could convince anyone that we weren't trying to set a record. We just ate our fill.

Chapter 7.7 Loss of Weight and Mid-section inches

The fitness staff at the FBI National Academy generally, and Al Beccaccio specifically, took great pride in the number of pounds and inches lost by police officers attending the National Academy.

Our class lost more weight and inches than any previous session. Statistically, classmates lost 1,125 pounds and 34 *feet* from around the waist. Everyone in the class lost weight and inches except one - me. I ate more at the academy than I did in Puerto Rico, yet I expended about the same amount of energy, so I gained both weight and inches. Al Beccaccio just couldn't believe it. He told me that I did it just to spite him.

Chapter 7.8 The Last "No Pain – No Gain" Class

The 140th Session ended the last physical fitness class with style and panache. They refused to dress out in gym clothes, refused to exercise, and dumped the instructors into the swimming pool, clothes and all. It was our way of saying thanks and good bye.

Bob and I made arrangements for our wives to travel to the FBI Academy for the Graduation Ball that was held the night before graduation. After the graduation ceremony, I packed my gear, said my goodbyes to classmates, and then Patsy and I headed for Washington D.C. for a couple of days of vacation. And just like that, it was over.

I headed for Naval Submarine Base San Diego, while Patsy returned to Naval Station Roosevelt Roads to pack our household goods for the move back to the States.

Saying goodbye to the Fitness Staff

Bob & Pat Bruckner
(Photos by John Cline)

CHAPTER EIGHT

Chapter 8.1 Naval Submarine Base San Diego (SUBASE)

If my tour at Naval Station Roosevelt Roads, Puerto Rico was my best duty assignment, (and it was), then Naval Submarine Base, San Diego was my least favorite. Not at first, but the last year or so was absolutely miserable, thanks to the executive officer.

I arrived at Naval Submarine Base, San Diego (SUBASE) late in March of 1985. The previous security officer had already gone to his next duty assignment, so there was no contact relief, and he wasn't all that thrilled at taking phone calls from me. There were four special projects designed to upgrade security, including an alarm and closed circuit television system (CCTV) to protect the weapons area where torpedoes and other munitions were stored. All four of the special projects had serious flaws, but none as grievous as the alarm and CCTV package. I contacted the station civil engineer and explained my concerns. His answer was, "we can't change the design at this late stage in the purchasing process." A contract had been awarded, and construction had already begun.

The main flaw in the system was that the alarms and CCTV used microwave radio instead of wire to transmit both alarms and television in the event of an intrusion. In a separate, unrelated contract, many of the roads were being dug up for the purpose of laying new utility lines. The contractor said that he would lay the alarm and CCTV wire in the trenches along with the new utility lines at no cost to the Navy except for the wires. I saw this as an opportunity to correct a serious security flaw, but the Civil Engineer said that the contract could not be changed. By the time the construction was completed, the commanding officer and the civil engineer had been rotated out of SUBASE.

I wrote a memo to the new commanding officer, Captain Ralph Johnson, outlining the weaknesses in the security system, but even if he wanted to repair the flaws, there was no funding. That memo saved me from a great deal of future grief.

Two years after I left SUBASE, the civilian security officer at SUBPAC (Submarine Force U.S. Pacific Fleet), the SUBASE parent command, filed a fraud, waste, and abuse report with NCIS alleging that I had wasted Navy funds by designing and implementing a security system with serious flaws. When the NIS Special Agent arrived to take my statement, I met him at the door with a copy of my memo.

His comment was, "Oh, you really did try to fix the problem."

I invited him into the office, but he said that he did not need to take a statement since he had a copy of my memo.

Security on SUBASE was a joke. Police cars were in such bad shape that they were being used as spare parts for cars belonging to other naval facilities in the San Diego area, which of course did nothing for SUBASE. Since the cars were repaired at Naval Station San Diego, there was little that could be done. Rather than send a police vehicle to Naval Station San Diego for maintenance, some of our police officers actually paid for minor repairs like oil changes and worn windshield wipers out of their own pocket, or they would repair the cars themselves. Otherwise, we would have had no cars for security use on the SUBASE, and nobody seemed to care.

There were no plans for response to acts of terrorism on the base. Police officers got very little firearms training, and there was no budget for ammunition. Morale was very low as police petty officers correctly assumed that nobody cared. Every cent on the SUBASE went for supporting the crews of submarines.

The barracks at SUBASE were better than those on most bases, yet when the crewmembers of a submarine damaged rooms, it was viewed as merely submariners having fun. They did a lot of damage. If a complaint was not filed, there was nothing the police could do. It was "out of my purview," I was told by the outgoing commanding officer.

Chapter 8.2 A Call from Puerto Rico

One morning in December 1985, I received a call asking me to report immediately to the captain's office. As I entered, the captain said that he was on the phone with the office of the Chief of Naval Operations who was patching a telephone call for me from Puerto Rico. When the phone patch was connected, Captain Mezzadri said that he had the Naguabo mayor, assistant mayor, chief of police, and other officials who had demanded the captain contact me at my new duty station. He went through the CNO's office because he didn't have my phone number at SUBASE. I talked with the officials for a few minutes. All they wanted was to say, Merry Christmas. It was nice to know that I may have been out of sight, but I was not out of mind. What a wonderful group of people! Even the outgoing SUBASE Commanding Officer was impressed.

Chapter 8.3 A New CO

Over the next two years, we did improve security significantly. I established a line item in the budget for new police vehicles, increased training, established an Emergency Operations Center, and designed anti and counterterrorism plans The new commanding officer, Captain Ralph Johnson, supported my efforts and took an active interest in base security and law enforcement. In fact, he had a standing order that if a base police officer stopped a commissioned officer for drunk driving, he was to be called, day or night. Since he lived in Navy quarters on the base, he could be at the scene in a very few minutes. Captain Johnson never interfered with the police. Rather, he acted as a witness. If the commissioned officer who was stopped became abusive toward the police, Captain Johnson would identify himself and counsel the commissioned officer about his or her actions. His presence stopped a lot of harassment of the police, who were petty officers, and who were routinely subjected to verbal abuse by chiefs and commissioned officers. Captain Johnson was a supportive and friendly commanding officer. He believed in solving problems, not just addressing the symptoms of problems.

Chapter 8.4 Meeting With the Admiral about Parking

The admiral, who was the Commander, Naval Submarine Group, and his staff, had offices on SUBASE. However, because he was expected to go to sea, he also had offices on a submarine tender (a ship designed to repair submarines both in port and at sea). I had no reason to know the admiral since I wasn't on his staff. Technically, he didn't have anything to do with SUBASE as long as the base was providing the support needed for the submarines and the crews. In the admiral's mind, the single most important security problem on the base was parking.

As naval bases go, SUBASE San Diego is really very small. Its main road follows the contour of the coastline on the bay on the south side of Point Loma, a peninsula that juts out into the ocean from the city of San Diego. Point Loma has a long history. Ballast Point, near the tip end of the peninsula, is named for the rocks that were loaded onto sailing ships as ballast for the trip back to the east coast after they had dropped off cargo and passengers. Many of the ballast stones, I'm told, were used in Boston to build their famed cobblestone streets.

Point Loma is also the site of Fort Rosecrans, which by the late 1800s had a number of very powerful guns and cannon to protect the harbor in San Diego. Today, Fort Rosecrans is best known for its National Cemetery. It is open to the public, along with the Cabrillo Lighthouse and other visitor attractions. The fact that Point Loma is open to the public increased the risk to SUBASE.

The public road going to the Rosecrans National Cemetery intersects with a road that provides direct access to the SUBASE. The gatehouse, where police would examine the identification of personnel desiring access to SUBASE, was unmanned during daylight hours. So, anyone could drive onto the submarine base. This was a huge gap in security, which was caused by the lack of personnel. With Captain Johnson's help, we got the personnel we needed to man the gate twenty four hours a day.

Because SUBASE is so small, there were never enough parking spaces for the crews of submarines, tenders, residents, and personnel (military and civilian) who work on the base. One afternoon, I received a call from Captain Johnson, who asked me to meet him in front of the building. I grabbed my cover and went outside where the admiral sat behind the wheel of his official car. Captain Johnson was in the front passenger seat.

Captain Johnson said, "Get in."

I got in the back seat.

The admiral drove around the base pointing out places where we could add parking. Of course, being the admiral, he didn't have to concern himself with driver safety, the Model Traffic Ordinance, fire lanes, or anything else that pertained to driving on the base.

Captain Johnson dutifully took notes until I said, "Admiral, I'll make you a deal. I won't tell you how to run a Submarine Group if you don't tell me how to run public safety, including driving and parking on base." There was an ominous silence.

The Admiral jammed on the brakes leaving skid marks on the pavement.

"GET OUT – GET OUT OF THE CAR," he yelled.

I got out of the car and began walking back to the office when I heard the car backing up, again leaving skid marks on the pavement. For a second, I thought he was going to run over me.

"GET IN – GET IN THE CAR," he yelled.

I got in the back seat again. Not a word was said. He drove me back to the Security Office, and then continued up to the CO's office. He never mentioned parking again. But that was not to be my last meeting with the admiral.

Chapter 8.5 Radiological Exercises

There is a requirement to exercise the options for response to an accidental release of radioactive gases from nuclear submarines. An Emergency Operations Center (EOC) had been set up years earlier for the Group Commander in one of the buildings on the base. Captain Johnson called one morning and said to meet him at the Submarine Group EOC. I had to ask where it was located.

I quickly made my way to the SUB GROUP EOC. The admiral and his staff had already arrived and were waiting for someone to unlock the double doors. The admiral was getting very angry and still no one could find the key. There is very little time to waste when responding to a radioactive release. Every second is precious. So I did what police officers do in an emergency. I pushed my way through the gaggle of officers, past the admiral, and kicked in the door. The wood around the lock splintered and there was a loud (Craaaack), as the double doors sprang open.

You would have thought that I had fired a gun. Stunned faces looked at me incredulously. Even the admiral looked surprised. I entered the room, found my desk, and started to work. For a moment, the admiral and his staff just stood outside the EOC. Finally, they entered and took their places and hurriedly began focusing on the exercise.

Captain Johnson arrived a few minutes later. He took his seat next to me and asked, "What happened to the door?"

"I kicked it open when they couldn't find the key," I said.

"Oh," he said and then went about his work.

Periodically, I saw the admiral looking at me, and there was no joy in his eyes. During the hotwash (Lessons Learned) review of the exercise, there were some words about placement of the keys to the EOC. In the end, the admiral got the last laugh; they usually do. I was charged with the door repairs and the locks, about three hundred dollars' worth of repairs that I had to pay for out of my pocket, rather than from the security department budget.

Other than the locked doors, the exercise went very well. Submariners are professionals when it comes to responding to radiological emergencies. But the exercise was also phony. I ran into that same scenario years later when I was participating in radiological exercises with the U.S. Department of Energy in Idaho. The radioactive cloud was never allowed to leave the confines of the base. That meant that we didn't have the opportunity to work realistically with civilian Emergency Management officials from the City and County of San Diego. So, in the weeks that followed, I set up a line of communications that allowed the base police to work with city and county officials in future exercises, without disrupting traffic or unsettling residents near the base.

When the next exercise occurred, I arrived to find that the double doors were already wide open. There were about ten officers sitting around drinking coffee and telling sea stories. I asked them where the admiral and his staff were.

They responded by putting on blue ball caps, saying they were the evaluators and umpires, and they didn't know where the admiral was. But the clock was ticking on a dangerous situation, so I had to take action.

The reason that the admiral and his staff were not in the EOC was that they were responding from the tender, which meant that they had to take boats from the ship to pier. Then they had to walk from the pier to the EOC. In all, the evolution took about twenty minutes. That meant that I had to take command of the situation because no one in authority was in the EOC. Remember, in a radiological emergency, <u>every second counts</u>. Luckily, I had been schooled in radiological response by General Atomic when I worked for General Dynamic Astronautics. I started a shelter-in- place procedure, and had all of the submarines lock down and stop ventilation. By the time I had stopped traffic and got people inside buildings, the admiral and his staff arrived. He was surprised to see that I was only responder in the EOC.

With a "who the hell do you think you are" voice, the admiral questioned me on the actions that I had taken. Since I had followed the Submarine Group response procedures and guidelines, there was little he could say. Instead, he just grunted. He and the staff took their positions, and I went to my desk to handle security matters. Captain Johnson was away from the base when the no-notice exercise was initiated, so the executive officer came in to handle SUBASE matters. When the exercise was concluded, we held the usual hotwash. No mention was made about my participation in the command function of the exercise. That's fairly normal in the Navy. Do the job well and you get no credit because excellence is the expected standard. Screw up and watch out!

Captain Ralph (Bud) Johnson passed away on January 6, 2008. It was an honor and a pleasure to serve under him. And I miss him.

Chapter 8.6 Making Life Miserable

While Captain Johnson was still the commanding officer, our XO was rotated to his new command and we got a new executive officer. Like me, he was a limited duty officer. When my wife met him, she remarked that "...he looked like a "sleaze." And he did. He had a narrow black mustache and a shock of hair angled across his brow that made him look a little like Adolph Hitler.

Shortly before his arrival at SUBASE, a Navy lieutenant junior grade (LTJG) was assigned to work in the Security Department as the assistant security officer. She had previously been working in the Administrative Department for a year, and would now spend a year gaining experience running a security department.

She was a graduate of the Naval Academy and went to great lengths to keep herself in good physical condition. She could outrun most of the police officers, and she could probably take most of them in a fight too. One day she entered my office and asked if she could talk with me privately.

I said, "Yes," and she closed the door and took a seat.

She told me that the new XO had sexually harassed her in a bar off the base. She indicated that she didn't want to file formal charges, but wanted to know what she should do in case he continued to sexually harass her.

I explained that in court, facts had a way of becoming distorted; especially facts regarding incidents that had occurred in the distant past. I advised her to write a letter outlining exactly what had happened. I suggested that a copy of the letter be given to me, although I would not open the letter until she asked me to, or unless the matter came up in court. I also suggested that she send a copy of the letter to someone whom she trusted, asking that person not to open the letter until it was necessary. At least that way, her frame of mind, and the facts as she knew them, would be in writing soon after the event had occurred. It wasn't foolproof, but it might be of some help should the incident go to trial.

For two weeks, I fretted over what I should do with the verbal information that I had been given. Not only was I the security officer, but I was also the designated Sexual Harassment Officer. What then was my duty in such a case? Finally, I went to Captain Johnson and told him that I had been apprised of sexual harassment by the XO. He was surprised, but said he would take care of it. The end of the problem, right? No, just the beginning.

A couple of days later, the XO called me to his office and told me he was going to ruin me and my naval career. Weeks later, after Captain Johnson left for a new assignment in the Pentagon and after we got a new CO, I was relieved of my duties as security officer.

I was given an office in the old morgue, a basement in one of the buildings that had once been a hospital during the First World War. The granite walls were so wet that a ball point pen would not write on paper in the office space. I had no computer or office equipment. My job was to write a new Emergency Management Plan because twice before, I had severely criticized a plan that had been developed by a contractor, who it turned out, was a personal friend of the XO. My criticism stemmed from the fact that the plan required about 500 people, while we only had about 350 people assigned to the base.

I have no idea how much the XO paid for the plan, but it was worthless as written. I asked the XO if he would mind if I worked at home, where I had a computer. He indicated that he didn't care where I worked. So I started working on the plan at home. I never finished.

I received a telephone call from the security officer detailer in Washington DC.

"How would you like to go to Bahrain and to the Persian Gulf for six months?" he asked.

"I'd love to," I answered. "I'll let you know," he said.

That was the last I heard from him until he called days later saying, "Your plane leaves in two hours."

He faxed my orders and I called Patsy at work. I couldn't tell her where I was going or how long I would be gone, but I said, "Don't plan on me for dinner for quite a while."

The assignment only delayed the sexual harassment trial. Even though I was on temporary orders to the Persian Gulf, I was still attached to the SUBASE, and would have to return following completion of my temporary duty.

Chapter 8.7 Bahrain and the Persian Gulf

I left San Diego by commercial air out of Lindbergh Field on the afternoon of October 28, 1987 and landed at London's Gatwick Airport on the morning of the 29th. Rod and Trish Kelley, with whom I had served in Puerto Rico, met me at the airport. This was to be a meet and greet at the airport only. However, my flight was late arriving, and I was unable to make the connection with the Cathay Pacific flight to Bahrain. I stayed overnight with Rod and Trish in Gosport, England. Rod was on exchange duty with a Chaplain from the British Royal Navy. I caught an afternoon flight to Bahrain, arriving at 1:00 a.m. on the 31st.

The outgoing Regional Security Officer, Wally Latall, (now Walter J. Latall, Lieutenant, USN, Retired) and Hamza, a Bahraini employed by the Navy to coordinate all manner of issues with local officials, met me at the airport. Hamza was very good at his job. I cleared Customs without having to open my luggage and was driven to a hotel where I caught a couple of hours of sleep before meeting with Admiral Bernson, who was the Commander, Middle East Force. My body had not yet adjusted to the time change and I kept dozing off during the meeting. I apologized for dozing off, but Admiral Bernson was very understanding, telling me that it would take a couple of days to adjust to the time change.

The admiral and his staff occupied spaces on the *USS LaSalle*

(AGF-3), but I was to stay ashore.

I would work out of the Administrative Support Unit (ASU) and would live in one of the hotels in town. Although I would function as the Navy's Regional Security Officer (RSO), I would wear civilian clothes except when I was aboard the ship or attending a military function. My boss was a Marine Corps colonel, but I had unfettered access to the admiral whenever I needed to talk with him.

My job was simple: Protect U.S. personnel, their dependents, British nationals, and naval resources ashore, including ships, when moored, in coordination with officials of the host country and U.S. Embassies throughout the Gulf region.

Note: Admiral Hal Bernson and the Earnest Will operation was prominently mentioned the book <u>Shadow Warriors </u>by Tom Clancy.

(Official Navy Photo)

The *USS La Salle* was painted white to reflect the Persian Gulf heat, which commonly reached over 130 degrees Fahrenheit. Because of the white paint, the ship became known as "**the Great White Ghost of the Arabian Coast**."

As the *USS La Salle* was the admiral's flagship, it stayed moored in port at Mina Sulman in Bahrain most of the time. It also stayed in port a lot because Congress and the Navy were not supporting Persian Gulf operations (known as the Tankers War) very well.

There was precious little funding for fuel. That would be a recurring theme throughout my tour of duty. The Joint Task Force, Middle East staff even tried to take my return ticket to San Diego so that they could cash it in to get money for fuel. When I complained, the Staff Judge Advocate General advised against that action, because the ticket had been purchased by SUBASE, not the Middle East Force. They did, however, take my rental car, saying I could drive a car assigned to the Chief of Staff when the staff was at sea, which wasn't very often. The rest of the time I had to walk or catch a taxi, which was not reimbursed.

Admiral Bernson took me to the American Embassy to meet with Ambassador Sam Zakhem and to get my embassy identification card. The ambassador was an extremely pleasant fellow. As he was giving me a brief about Bahrain and the royal family, there was something that both he and the admiral said that bothered me.

Speaking of Arab officials in general, he said, "They love us."

I had my doubts. I met the Embassy's Regional Security Officer, received my ID card, and made an appointment to meet with the CIA Station Chief the next day. The admiral and I returned to the ship and then I went on to the ASU to meet the commanding officer, XO, security officer, NIS agents, and to look over my new office.

The next morning, I met with the CIA Station Chief. When I mentioned NIS, he went into a verbal rage that ended with his saying, "I won't have anything to do with them."

The NIS agents had been gathering intelligence, which he viewed to be his exclusive fiefdom. He didn't give me any useful information, basically saying that everything was cool. I still had my doubts. NIS didn't give me any useful information either.

Chapter 8.8 Operations Earnest Will (July 1987 – Dec 1988) and Prime Chance (Aug 87 – June 89)

Iran and Iraq had been at war since the early 1980s. By the mid-1980s, Iran began attacking Kuwait's oil tankers because Kuwait was a non-combatant ally of Iraq. Mainly for Cold War strategic reasons and to protect national interests, the United States sent ships into the Persian Gulf to ensure that sea lanes remained open to international shipping. Although the U.S. took a neutral position in the Iran-Iraq war, it became more involved when an Iraqi jet fighter sent two Exocet missiles into the hull of the USS Stark (FFG-31), killing thirty seven sailors, and wounding a great many more. The frigate had been on patrol in the Persian Gulf about fifty miles off the coast of Bahrain when it was attacked; the ship was clearly in international waters.

Consequently, the United States agreed to reflag several of the Kuwaiti oil tankers, making them in effect U.S. ships. In July 1987, Operation Earnest Will was implemented. This required the U.S. Navy to escort Kuwaiti oil tankers through the Persian Gulf and the Strait of Hormuz into to the Indian Ocean for transit to global markets. A month later, Operation Prime Chance, involving Navy SEALs and Army Special Operations personnel and equipment was initiated to support of the Navy's Earnest Will mission.

In July 1987, a reflagged super-tanker, the SS Bridgeton, was struck by a mine while being escorted by U.S. Navy war ships. Although Iran was suspected of laying the mines, there was no proof until the Iran Ajr was captured by Navy SEALs with Army Special Forces helicopter support. Mining gulf-waters added a new dimension to the "Tankers War."

Chapter 8.9 Rethinking in-port Security

If there was a wartime mentality while at sea (and there was,) that same attitude was greatly diminished in Bahrain, which was viewed as a safe harbor. To keep it that way, the Navy brought in the Marine Mammal Unit to patrol the port of Mina Sulman where U.S. ships were moored. The Mammal Unit personnel laid out a designated area for the dolphins to patrol, looking for swimmers who might try to attach explosives to the hull of the vessels being protected. If and when the dolphins alerted handlers to a suspected presence, Recon Marines would enter the water to deal with the attackers. Since port security was one of my responsibilities, I became the Liaison Officer between the Mammal Unit and the admiral's staff.

Another group in Bahrain was an Explosive Ordnance Disposal (EOD) team who maintained a capability to disarm Nuclear Improvised Explosive Devices (NIED) as well as other types of explosive devices, including sea mines. I ran interference for them, as much as I could.

Iranians were laying contact sea mines. When U.S. warships saw a mine, they began the practice of shooting at the horns on the mine to blow up the mine while it was at a perceived safe distance from the ship. More times than not, shooters hit the metal casing of the mine, which then filled with sea water, resulting in the mine sinking to the bottom of the shallow gulf. As the mine travelled with the currents, there was a risk that a mine's horn would come in contact with the sea floor and detonate. Should a ship be on the surface over the mine when it exploded, the blast and concussion could break the ship's back, or at the very least, cause severe damage to the ship and it's personnel.

The EOD team leader asked me to get with the admiral and see if there was some way to stop ships' personnel from shooting at the mines. Rather, he said it was much safer for his men to swim to the mine and detonate it in a controlled environment. I ran into a lot of opposition when I took the EOD team's methodology to the staff, but eventually, we got to the point where EOD was called when a mine was found. They disarmed a lot of sea mines.

My biggest problem was that I didn't speak Arabic or Farsi. Iranians don't consider themselves to be Arabs. Rather, they are Persian and speak Farsi.

There were two Marine Corps Intelligence warrant officers who had a mission that kept them primarily in Bahrain. They were language specialists who spoke both Arabic and Farsi, and they needed a place in which to work. I had an office and I needed translators. We cut a deal: they worked out of my office, and they would translate information from Arabic and Farsi to English.

I often carried a micro-cassette tape recorder with me. I would record conversations in public places that sounded like political debate by local townspeople. The recordings were translated by the Marines. The recordings paid off. Our presence in the Gulf was not as well accepted by the Shiite community in Bahrain as we had been led to believe by the CIA Station Chief and NIS.

Using the recordings, coupled with an in-depth analysis of the political history of Persian Gulf countries, I wrote a report which I took to the CIA Station Chief. We met in his secluded chambers of the embassy. He read the first page and flew into a rage.

"You're collecting intelligence," he charged.

"No, I said. "I wouldn't even know how to go about doing that. My job requires that I establish a vulnerability baseline, to determine the terrorist threat by conducting a physical security threat assessment."

He couldn't argue with that, so he asked, "What do you want me to do with the report?"

I responded by saying that I would be meeting with the admiral in the morning, and that I was giving the CIA agent an advanced copy for use any way he deemed appropriate.

The next morning, the admiral started the meeting by saying, "Before we get started, I think you should read this new report from the CIA."

Word-for-word, it was my report. I didn't mind not getting credit for it. Having the CIA endorse my work gave it more credence. Where naval facilities in the gulf had been at a low terrorist threat condition, I recommended that the admiral immediately move to a high threat condition.

That meant that security would be tightened to include inspecting vehicles for bombs and checking outgoing vehicles for the removal of government property. That takes time and personnel, and slows the traffic pattern significantly. It wasn't a popular move, but it was the proper thing to do in a quasi-war zone.

Chapter 8.10 Preparing to Evacuate American Citizens

One of the contingencies that the State Department worries about is how to evacuate American citizens (non-military personnel) from host countries when the level of political activity places Americans at widespread risk of injury or death.

The first method that embassies of all nations turn to is the use of commercial transportation; aircraft, buses, and ships. The trick to using those methods of transportation is to get an early enough start on the evacuation process to ensure that transportation will be available. The State Department will sometimes contract with airlines and ships. As the risk increases, commercial transportation becomes less and less available. In the Gulf, it was decided that U.S. Navy ships would be used to evacuate American citizens if commercial transportation was not available.

Even if the embassies do get an early start on the evacuation process, they have to try to contact every known American in the country and give them instructions as to where to go, how to get there, and more importantly, when to get there. Periodically, embassy personnel exercised the process. My boss, the Marine colonel, and I attended the exercises representing the Navy. As the Navy's Regional Security Officer, I also provided the terrorism input to exercise scenarios. The tabletop exercises took all day and they were intense. It wasn't unusual for tempers to flare.

Every embassy staff member took seriously his or her evacuation responsibilities. I am convinced that they would (and will) save many American civilian and dependent lives in the event that an evacuation becomes necessary.

Even the ambassadors participated in the exercises. They, too, took their decisions and role-playing seriously. In short, embassy staffs performed well beyond my expectations.

Embassy Staff during an Evacuation Exercise
(Photo by John Cline)

Chapter 8.11 Working with the Brits

The British have had an influence in the Middle East for hundreds of years. Bahrain had a heavy influence of Brits while I was there. The school attended by American dependents was run by the Brits. It was decided that should an evacuation be required, we would cooperate with the British government and remove as many British citizens as we could along with Americans. Because terrorism was a growing concern, I was detailed to work with the school to improve their physical and antiterrorism security.

Much of the information that I received about implementing security in the Gulf came from Mike Borne, the Director of Security for the Port of Mina Sulman. He was a former Special Air Service (SAS) commando. The SAS is the Special Forces arm of the British Army, and they are expert in counterterrorism. He had a saying that served me well. He said, "Arabs have thirty ways of saying yes, but only one of them really means yes." I learned what he meant the hard way. I negotiated several security agreements with host national officials only to have them fail to show up. They almost never said, "NO," but many times, yes meant no.

As the investigation into the attack on the USS Stark wound up, the scuttlebutt around the ASU was that the Iraqi pilot of the F-1 Mirage that fired on the USS Stark may have been a Brit. If true, that would not have been unusual. There were many Brit pilots flying for Middle Eastern countries, both in a commercial and military capacity. Evidently, tapes of the incident revealed that the voice of the Mirage pilot had a distinctly British accent.

The Brits were fun to work with. Every Thursday afternoon, the Hash House Harriers sponsored a run. The H3, a name by which they are sometimes known, is an international club for running and for drinking alcoholic beverages.

In Bahrain, the Hash was started in 1972 and they have now celebrated over 1800 runs. This is not a race. It is a run. And its members often said that they were a "drinking club with a running problem."

The Hash is not about running around a track, nor is it without purpose. Loosely, it follows the game rules of hound and hare: Hares lay out the running trail that the rest of the hashers (hounds) follow. There may be false trails, shortcuts and even trail breaks all designed to keep as much of the pack together as is possible, regardless of physical capability. Markings used to identify the trail are called "hash marks."

There was always plenty of beer at trail's end. In Bahrain's 100 plus degree heat, there was also the traditional block of ice to sit on as after-run ceremonies took place. In short, the Hash was a way to promote physical fitness, get rid of existing hangovers, acquire a voracious thirst, and to convince old timers that just maybe they weren't as old as they thought. This is the kind of fun that you would expect from a college frat party. It isn't any wonder they forgot how old they were.

Chapter 8.12 Tensions Rise in the Gulf

Not everything was fun and games, so we had to take the good times anytime we could. Iran's gunboats frequently attacked tankers and escorts, especially in the northern Gulf and in the Strait of Hormuz, which is only a little over twenty miles wide.

Saudi Arabia and Kuwait did not want U.S. forces in their countries, so to respond quickly to the Iranian threats to tankers and escorts in the northern Gulf, the U.S. positioned two large barges in the gulf between Iraq and Iran. The barges, Wimbrown VII (250 by 70 feet), and the smaller Hercules served as floating bases. Special Boat Units with Mark Three Patrol Boats, and some smaller boats provided support for two SEAL platoons and the Army's special operations helicopter unit known as the "Night Stalkers." The first helicopter operations took place in October 1987 when the Night Stalkers sank three

Iranian patrol boats. Over the next few months, intense fighting took place involving all of the various Special Forces units assigned to the barges. The barges were moved every few days so that they wouldn't become static targets.

Chapter 8.13 The Bob Hope Show

On December 23rd, 1987 the admiral called me to his office onboard the USS La Salle.

"Bob Hope and his cast will arrive on Christmas Day," he said.

I was to coordinate security. The Bahrain Government wouldn't allow us to hold the Christmas show ashore, so we had to hold the show on the *USS Okinawa*. Although there was no specific threat to Bob Hope or to the cast, the admiral wanted to be sure that security was particularly effective. No one wanted to become known for having lost Bob Hope while he was on a USO tour.

The cast would arrive at the Navy's Aviation Unit at Bahrain International Airport. They would be transported by bus to boats waiting at the port of Mina Sulman for a short trip to the *USS Okinawa*. The plan called for the cast being at the airport for no more than thirty minutes. A police escort was to escort the buses to the Port of Mina Sulman.

The Bahrain Police formed an outer perimeter, ensuring that unauthorized personnel did not enter the area. Bahrain's counterterrorism unit formed an inner perimeter in case someone did get through the police boundary. Heavily armed Navy police and SEALs were in the hangar in case of an attack.

When the cast arrived in Bahrain, they absolutely refused to go to the *USS Okinawa* by boat. The Navy liaison officer who traveled with the Bob Hope Show said that the cast got seasick when they took boats to the *USS Enterprise* in the Gulf of Oman, and that there was no way that they would take boats to the *USS Okinawa*. What was Plan B? We didn't have a Plan B.

There was one helicopter available (Desert Duck One). We loaded the cast members who wanted to fly on the helicopter. Because the helicopter could only carry five passengers, It would take three or more hours before we could get the entire cast of eighty people to the ship. To save time, the rest of the cast, including Bob Hope, decided to ride the boats to the *USS Okinawa*.

We drove to the pier with our police escort and boarded the boats for the short trip to the *USS Okinawa*. Six foot waves bounced the boats up and down as we approached the ladder on the side of the ship. Bob Hope couldn't get the rhythm to make the transition from the small liberty boat to the ladder, so as a wave carried us upward, I grabbed Bob Hope around the waist and swung him over the boat's gunwale to the landing at the bottom of the ladder. I noticed that he was really quite frail.

A security boundary was established around the *USS Okinawa* using patrol boats and personnel from the Special Boat Unit, Marine Mammal Unit, Recon Marines, and three mine sweepers. Two of the mine sweepers were assigned to patrol the outer perimeter, outside the mouth of the harbor. Another MSO was assigned to patrol the inner harbor. The EOD Unit spent a major part of the day inspecting the hull of the *USS Okinawa,* and they confirmed that there were no mines attached to the ship.

They made periodic patrols with the Special Boat Unit, and remained on standby until the cast left late the next day and after the *USS Okinawa* had once again put to sea.

I had an "all access" USO pass, so I could go through the cast's quarters, which was off limits to the ship's crew. Even though I had access to the stars, there was very little time for idle conversation.

U.S. Ambassador Sam Zachem and Admiral
Bernson (Photo by John Cline)

The first show took place at 2200 and it was great, as you would expect. The second show took place at 1400 on the day after Christmas.
The first show was for military personnel, but the second show included many of the civilians and dependents who worked and lived in
Bahrain.

The cast stayed on the ship overnight. However, the next day, after
the second show, the officer's wives of the admiral's staff invited twenty-six of the eighty cast members to join them for a tour of the souq
(Bahrain's version of a shopping mall). I couldn't follow all twenty-six
cast members, so I chose to stay with Admiral Bernson, the ambassador, and Mr. Hope.

Mr. Hope and the cast were scheduled to fly out at 2300. Passenger loading was to commence at 2200. The Bahraini government did not allow us to keep the U.S. Air Force planes in Bahrain overnight, so Ambassador Sam Zachem made arrangements for the planes to fly to another Gulf nation for the night. The aircraft returned at 1800 to load the stage equipment and to conduct the preflight inspection for the next leg of the trip.

About 2130, the admiral and Bob Hope went to the Aviation Unit at Bahrain International Airport where most of the cast was already busy loading the aircraft. As Mr. Hope and Admiral Bernson talked, we counted noses and noticed that Barbara Eden was not with the cast.

Suddenly, a rather sizable contingent of the Bahraini royal family arrived and Bob Hope was introduced to each of the family members. Passenger loading time came and went; still no Barbara Eden. I was worried.

The last time she had been seen, she was in the souq. Nobody could remember when or how she had left. About thirty minutes after the scheduled passenger loading time, a royal family prince drove up to the plane in his Rolls Royce, and there in the passenger seat sat Barbara Eden. Everyone, except me, was all smiles. Barbara Eden and the prince said their goodbyes. She boarded the plane and off they went, right on schedule at 2300. Man, was I relieved! The various elements of the security detail stood down and I thanked them for their around the clock service. They had done an exceptional job on very short notice.

Since I had been working for two days and two nights, I just wanted to go to bed. Merry Christmas!

Bob Hope aboard the *USS Okinawa*
December 26, 1987 (Photo by John Cline)

Chapter 8.14 Physical Security Surveys for Ports

Monday, February 8, 1988 found me flying out of Bahrain International Airport enroute to Abu Dhabi in the United Arab Emirates. I was the only non-Arab on the plane. About forty Arabs in the coach class compartment got into a fist fight. I just wanted to keep from getting punched.

On arrival in Abu Dhabi, I attended a short meeting, followed by a trip to Dubai. After spending the night in Dubai, it was off to Fujairah to conduct a port security survey.

My room at the Hilton Hotel in Dubai.
Beds were only about a foot high.
(Photo by John Cline)

The road to Fujairah was straight as an arrow. After a number of miles there would be a roundabout for no apparent reason. I don't remember what the speed limit was, or if there was one, but there were few cars on the road, so driving over 100 miles per hour was acceptable. The greatest hazard was hitting a herd of camels crossing the road. My driver said that on the average of once each month, the driver, and front seat passenger of speeding cars were killed when they hit a camel because they couldn't stop in time. I looked at the speedometer.

We were travelling at well over 100 MPH (not kilometers) miles per hour.

Camel herd crossing the road
(Photo by John Cline)

I met with the harbor master, Captain Roger G. Turnbull, regarding port security. The port was very modern, and the harbor master took pride in the port's cargo handling. As ports go, it was immaculate.

There was little in the way of security; no patrol boats or trained personnel to respond to an attack. Foothills broke the flat desert landscape about a half mile inland from the port facility. I wanted to view the port from the foothills, but there was no road. The local Sheik provided us with transportation—camels. After riding to and from the foothills, I can honestly say that I really do not like riding camels. Based on the tracks that I found, the desert behind the foothills was routinely travelled by Bedouins and by local residents on wadi-busters (quads).

I returned to the port facility later that night. It was lit up like a Christmas tree. In the darkness, it was possible to easily see (and shoot) personnel on the pier without being seen on the dark desert floor.

The port facility was close to the main road, and it would have been simple for a terrorist group to drive to the area with shoulder fired missiles and attack a ship that was refueling or loading provisions, especially at night. It would have been even easier for the Iranians to attack the facility from the gulf using their Swedish-made Boghammers.

Following the night check of the port facility, I was invited to dinner with the local sheik and a number of local dignitaries. We had chilled sheep's brain and sheep's tongue. UGH!

The next morning, I continued my security inspection of the beach area along the Gulf. My two guides, one of whom spoke broken English, followed behind. As we were walking down the beach, I suddenly heard the sound of a bolt being cycled on a fifty caliber machine gun. I froze and looked toward the sound. A soldier was sitting behind a tripod mounted machine gun, which was pointed at me. I swear he had a grin on his face.

I looked back at my guides. They had stopped some twenty- five feet behind me.

The guide who could speak broken English said, "One more step and he will shoot you."

One more step and I would have illegally entered Oman. There was no sign, just a soldier with a machine gun.

Later that morning, I met the USS Carr where I provided a port security brief to the crew. It was their first tour in the Persian Gulf. After the briefing, I had to hire a car and driver to take me back to Abu Dhabi for the flight to Bahrain. Although I had an international driver's license, it hadn't been stamped with authorization to drive in the United Arab Emirates.

My Guides – who watched to see if I would
be shot! (Photo by John Cline)

Chapter 8.15 One Major Faux Pas

At 1500 on February 27, 1988, Admiral Tony Less took command
as Commander, Joint Task Force Middle East. Whoever wrote the
invitations for the change of command ceremony addressed them
to the sheik and sheika (wife of the sheik). Although it is customary
to invite the wives of officials in western cultures, it isn't acceptable in the Muslim culture. One sheik was particularly offended, and
because I was based ashore, I was selected to apologize for the command's mishandling of the invitations.

I arrived at the sheik's office, and was ushered inside where
I began the apologetic litany. I was lambasted for nearly thirty
minutes about how dumb Americans are about the Muslim reli-
gion and customs of the nations throughout the Persian Gulf. Of
course, the official was a member of the royal family, so all I could

do was to take the criticism without appearing to be angry. I was seething.

Finally, after the sheik had vented his anger toward Americans in general and me in particular, I was allowed to leave. He didn't bother to shake my hand when offered.

The invited sheiks gathered at the change of command ceremony aboard the USS Coronado (AGF-11), which had earlier replaced the USS La Salle as the admiral's flagship. They apparently had a good time. Even the sheik who had been particularly offended by the wording of the invitations seemed to enjoy the occasion. Of course, none of the wives attended. If anything was said about the invitations, I didn't know about it. My job was to provide the security for the event, coordinating military and civilian police, the private security of each sheik, and the Bahraini counterterrorism force.

I was nervous about the number of people carrying guns; everyone seemed to have their own private security detail. But we got through it without incident.

The new admiral's staff was made up of higher ranking officers. Where lieutenants and lieutenant commanders had been the backbone of the planning staff under Admiral Bernson, under Admiral Less, there were a gaggle of commanders and captains, each with their own individual egos. The lieutenants and lieutenant commanders, who had been doing the job for a couple of years, were now no longer department heads. They were returned to junior officer status. There was tension on the staff. Since I worked ashore, I was pretty much unaffected. The Marine colonel who had been my boss under Admiral Bernson was still my boss under Admiral Less, and we got along well. Admiral Less, like Admiral Bernson, was a joy to work with.

The month of March saw me travelling around the gulf attending meetings with various officials and security personnel while conducting port security physical security inspections. Although March was not particularly exciting, April was something else.

To LT John Cline,
Thanks for
a Great job
here in the
Joint Task
Force
Tony Less
RADM USN
CJTFME

Admiral Less, Commander, Joint Task Force
Middle East (Official Navy Photo)

Chapter 8.16 Full Alert at the ASU

On April 12th, the Bahraini police notified us that they had received a report that five men in uniforms with automatic weapons had been observed in the vicinity of the Administrative Support Unit. That and other information indicated that the ASU would be attacked that night. We recalled all of the security personnel, armed them with automatic weapons and the few night vision devices that we had, and waited for the attack.

Although I was concerned about snipers from buildings that had a height advantage, I was more concerned that one of our security personnel might shoot a civilian pedestrian because the security personnel were so hyped up with talk of an attack. I walked down the middle of the streets of the ASU, talking continuously with security personnel by radio, trying to keep them alert while simultaneously telling them to keep their finger off the trigger until an attack actually occurred. The attack never came. I can't say that the full alert prevented the attack, but we were ready if it had come. Four days later, the ASU Security Officer suffered an attack of appendicitis and had to be hospitalized. I took over his duties as well as my own.

Chapter 8.17 *USS Samuel B. Roberts* (FFG-58) Hit by a Mine

Several of the officers from the ASU were going to a goat grab. They were looking forward to an evening of frivolity on April 14th. At 1700 the pagers started going off. The *USS Roberts* had been hit by a mine while at sea in the gulf.

The first report indicated there were four injuries, two burn victims and two with back injuries. Medical doctors assigned to Bahrain were immediately recalled to fly to the *USS Roberts*. In all, ten sailors were evacuated because of injuries. Six of the injured sailors were able to return to the ship. However four burn victims were sent to hospitals in the States.

The ship was barely afloat. Quick thinking and sustained action by the crew saved her. The crew fought fires and flooding for over six hours. One sailor told me that the crew had held the ship together with steel cable that they wrapped around deck cleats near the bow and stern of the ship, literally pulling the ship together around the fifteen foot hole that the mine had created.

Divers recovered unexploded sea mines in the area where the *USS Roberts* had been hit. They discovered that the serial numbers on the unexploded mines matched the series of serial numbers from mines that had been seized months earlier on the Iran Ajr; proof positive that Iran was behind the mining. Those of us in the gulf were anxious to strike back.

Technically, the United States was not at war with Iran; any response would have to be a measured response, authorized only by the President of the United States.

Chapter 8.18 Operation Praying Mantis

Iranian oil platforms were being used to control attacks on oil tankers and U.S. warships. In response to the mining of international waters and for the damage to the *USS Roberts*, the President directed that U.S. forces take out two of the nearly one hundred Iranian oil platforms. The two targeted platforms, *Sirri* and *Sassan*, were hit on April 18th in operation Praying Mantis.

Oil platforms are not merely pumping stations; they are the nerve centers of oil fields. Taking out a platform means that the oil produced from that oil field can't be sold on the world market until extensive apparatus is repaired. The *Sirri* platform is located on Sirri Island, best described as a small atoll. *Sassan* is actually seven platforms anchored to the seabed, and tethered together by a series of catwalks.

> My notes regarding the attacks differ somewhat from news media reports, so I will cite the information that I hastily wrote down, and some of the information that I was given verbally. I don't know which is the more accurate, so I will call this an unofficial version.

At 0700, U.S. destroyers *USS Merrill* and *USS Lynde McCormick* approached the oil platform *Sassan*, making known by radio their intentions to destroy the platform. Iranians on the platform were asked to leave immediately.

Simultaneously, Marines from the *USS Trenton* on Sea Knight helicopters circled the *Sassan* Oil Platform. Two Cobra gunships provided air support. A number of Zodiac inflatable boats with Navy SEALs approached the platform from the sea.

The Iranians fired at one of the Cobras with a high powered rapid fire gun from what was described as a barracks. The Cobra gunships fired a couple of missiles into the barracks area while Marines, including the two Marine intelligence officers who worked out of my office, rappelled onto the burning platforms. SEAL teams attacked from beneath the system of platforms. As the Marines and SEALs spread out across the platforms, the Iranians jumped into the sea and evacuated the area on small boats.

For two hours, SEALs and Marines gathered a large number of intelligence documents and several SAM-7 missiles. The platforms proved to be heavily armed fortresses, as well as command and control centers. SEALs and Marines placed well over 1, 000 pounds of explosives around the complex, which was detonated by the SEALs after the Marines were once again airborne.

At 0720 frigates USS Simpson and USS Bagley and the cruiser USS Wainwright served a similar warning to the Iranian crew on the Sirri platform. When most of the Iranians had evacuated the platform, the U.S. ships began shelling the complex with five inch 38 and 94 caliber guns. When an Iranian tug boat arrived on scene, shelling stopped until the oil rig crew could safely be evacuated. In all, over ninety rounds were fired into the oil platform complex.

Accounts of Operation Praying Mantis often refer to it as the largest naval surface engagement since the Second World War. Iran attacked U.S. ships with at least two frigates, missiles, fighter jets, and a number of patrol boats. It should be recognized that the attacks lasted most of the day, and into the early hours of the night. This was not a short battle. Rather, this was a coordinated series of attacks designed to rid the gulf of the entire U.S. battle group.

In the northern gulf, Iran fired Silkworm missiles at the two barges used by U.S. Special Forces. The missiles were diverted by chaff fired by the *USS Gray*. Iran also attacked the two barges with F-4 fighter jets and patrol boats, but both the fighter jets and the patrol boats turned back when they were "painted" by the *USS Gray's* fire control radar.

Meanwhile, in the southern and central parts of the gulf, the Iranian warship *Joshan*, a 147-foot missile patrol boat, fired missiles at U.S. ships that participated in the attack on the *Sirri* platform. The *USS Simpson* and *USS Wainwright* returned missile fire, sinking the *Joshan*. Numerous other attacks on civilian ships, naval vessels, and military aircraft were reported to have taken place throughout the day. Two Iranian frigates, the *Sahand* and the *Sabalan*, fired on U.S. vessels after ignoring several requests to leave the area. U.S. aircraft sank the *Sahand,* and severely damaged the *Sabalan*.

There were a large number of other attacks, but the reporting became so numerous that I had to stop taking notes. Finally, after nightfall, the attacks stopped.

It should also be noted that the Sirri and the Sassan oil platforms were not the first to be attacked by U.S. forces. Several months earlier, the president ordered the attack on another Iranian oil platform in retaliation for attacks on oil tankers. I don't remember the name of the platform, but it was destroyed by the EOD team that I worked with.

Chapter 8.19 A Short Look in the Rearview Mirror

I do have one observation. Years later, when talking with citizens of the United States, I have yet to meet anyone, not personally involved, who remembers the Tankers War, or any of the operations mentioned herein.

Iranian oil platform – Photo by EOD

It occurs to me that Americans can recall the plays and final scores of football games better than they remember the battles in which Americans were killed and maimed in defense of liberty, independence, freedom, and economic stability.

Chapter 8.20 What I Took With Me from Bahrain

At 0300 on April 25, 1988, I left Bahrain and the Persian Gulf on a commercial aircraft (Cathay Pacific Airways), which at that time was flown exclusively by Brits.

We flew out in a horrible thunderstorm that made for very rough flying weather. But as the pilot said over the public address system, "Flying in bad weather means there is less likelihood of being shot out of the sky by Iranian or Iraqi fighter jets."

You just got to love that Brit sense of humor. To lessen the odds even more, the pilot flew a route well away from Iraq and Iran. As the sun broke over the Swiss Alps, I realized how really tired I was from six months of operations.

Bahraini officials with whom I worked were very concerned about their place in the world, not just the on the planet, but within the Muslim world. If you were an Ambassador or Admiral they treated you extremely well, which prompted the feeling that "they love us." The rest of us were regarded more as a mercenary military force that was filling their need for stability in the Gulf Region, and which they regarded as paid servants, much like the foreign janitors, maids, cooks, and gardeners that they imported; a necessary evil. The royal family was terrified of Iran.

We were not allowed to fly the American flag on the ASU where it might be seen by those outside the facility. We could not practice Christian or Jewish religions on the base. Bahrainis did, however, turn a blind eye as we held Christian services on Sunday mornings in a private house just outside the base. It would be unfair to call Bahrain the Las Vegas of the Persian Gulf, although that label was commonly attributed to them. They were certainly the most liberal of Muslim Gulf nations that I visited. But they had a distorted view of Americans. For instance, they would not allow me to use ham radio in Bahrain because, in their opinion, all American amateur radio operators are spies.

I found the Brits, especially Mike Borne, to be the most practical of people. They knew more about dealing with Arab officials than we did. All too often, we didn't listen to the Brits. As well as being industrious, I found the Brits to be the most fun-loving people on the island. I left feeling a little sorry that I didn't get to participate with them more.

To the men and women of the United States Armed Forces who lived and worked in Bahrain during Operation Earnest Will, I have never met a more dedicated bunch of military and civilian personnel anywhere. I would gladly serve with them again. They were the equal of those with whom I served in Puerto Rico, and that is indeed high praise.

As the aircraft descended to Gatwick International Airport, I looked forward to seeing my wife, Pat, who had flown from San Diego to spend a week's leave with me in London. We were to meet Chaplain Rod Kelley and his wife Trish. Trisha's mother was diagnosed with cancer, so she had flown back to the states. Rod spent as much time as he could playing tour guide.

During my first hour in Great Britain, I was almost run over by a speeding car in a roundabout. I looked left when I should have looked right. Pat grabbed my coat and pulled me back just in the nick of time. After six months of operations in the Persian Gulf, I almost got wacked in London traffic. Just Great!

Chapter 8.21 The XO's Courts Martial

After a week of touring England, including a full day at Harrods Department Store, where Pat got to shop until I was ready to drop, we flew back to the states, collected our bags, and got in a long line waiting to go through U.S. Customs. The customs inspectors were checking everyone's luggage, so the process was taking a long, long time. Finally, we reached the head of the line.

I handed my official passport, tourist passport, and military identification to the customs inspector.

Pat handed over her passport. The inspector examined every page of my official passport, noting each gulf nation that I had entered and departed. He looked at my military identification and then looked me in the eye and said, "Welcome home, commander." Then he waved us through. We didn't have to open our jam-packed luggage. His gesture made me feel very proud of my service in the U.S. Navy. I noticed that others waiting in line were curious, maybe even jealous, as to why we didn't have to open our luggage. ☺

We got to San Diego after another day-long flight. We were exhausted, but the kids were excited to hear about the Middle East and our trip to England. I drove to the SUBASE and checked in.

The next morning, I checked to see what changes had taken place at the Security Department, noting that they were still following the procedures that I had implemented for physical security and antiterrorism. I reported to the captain's office. He didn't want to see me, so the administrative officer told me to go back on leave until after the executive officer's trial because nobody wanted me around the base.

I checked with my detailer by phone and he told me that I would be going to the USS Independence (CV-62), after the trial. The trial was to take place on May 26, 1988 at Naval Station San Diego. The legal beagles had held up the trial until I got back from the Persian Gulf. I had hoped they would hold the trial without me. No such luck!

Actually, the XO didn't have to go to a Court Martial. He could have opted for Admiral's Mast, which is similar to a Captain's Mast, and which is not a trial, but he believed strongly that he would not be convicted. He was the Navy's senior-most officer to be charged with sexual harassment at the time.

I arrived at the appointed hour, checked in with the Legal Office, and was directed to a waiting room adjacent to the courtroom. Several of the witnesses, including Captain Johnson, the former CO, were waiting to be called into the courtroom as witnesses.

The atmosphere was somber; no one, including me, wanted to be there. After nearly an hour of waiting, I was called to testify.

I was sworn in and seated. I looked into the faces of the jury, all commanders, and captains, and saw a decidedly hostile majority. It was an uncomfortable moment. The only person in the gallery was Tom Burgess, a well-known writer for the San Diego Union, who was taking notes for his story that would appear in the morning edition.

The Trial Counsel, who is the prosecutor, began his line of questions. Then the Defense questioned me. The main line of questioning from the Defense Attorney, and later by the jury, was whether or not I had called the Fraud, Waste, and Abuse Hotline in Washington. The question was asked several times in different ways.

Evidently, whoever called the Hotline had identified himself as a master chief petty officer with over 25 years of naval service. Although I was a lieutenant, I was a temporary grade lieutenant. I was also a permanent grade master chief. Everyone was convinced that it was I who had placed the call. I had been in the Persian Gulf when the call was made and frankly, I was a little busy with things more important than calling the hotline. I was, however, irked that questioning had more to do with WHO called the hotline instead of whether or not the XO had sexually harassed the lieutenant and several of the SUBASE enlisted female sailors. I was dismissed with a warning not to talk about my testimony or the trial to other witnesses.

The trial went on another day. Deliberations went into the night-time hours. Finally, a verdict was announced: "GUILTY."

When addressing the news media, the XO said only that he would "...never again attend another social function where there are female Navy officers or enlisted women. If you smile at someone today, it's all over." Even after being found guilty, he belittled the fact that he had fondled several women and kissed at least one enlisted woman.

The XO was found guilty on three of the four counts of sexual harassment. He was fined $3,600. He also received an official reprimand

and a reduction in seniority. The sentence was a mere slap on the wrist compared to what he could have gotten, including four years in prison, dismissal from the Navy, and the loss of all pay and allowances. He had gotten off nearly Scott-free, and he knew it. So did the admiral of Submarine Group Five, to whom the commanding officer of SUBASE reported.

The admiral held Admiral's Mast and charged the XO with Conduct Unbecoming an Officer. He reduced the XO from commander to lieutenant commander. The XO elected to appeal the admiral's punishment, and to retire from the Navy. I saw the XO several times over the next few weeks. Each time he would tell me that he was going to beat the reduction in rank. Within a few days of his retirement, when he would have beaten the ruling, his appeal came back denied. He retired as a lieutenant commander. In my opinion, some justice had at last been served.

Chapter 8.22 Hail and Farewell

Every command recognizes those officers who have recently reported aboard the ship or station, as well as the contributions made by departing officers at a Hail and Farewell ceremony. I was informed of the date, time, and place that SUBASE would hold my farewell, although I got the feeling that the caller wanted me to decline. I didn't, but the commanding officer did decline to attend.

Several officers had recently reported aboard SUBASE. Two officers were leaving – my assistant security officer, (who had been one of the victims of the XO's sexual harassment), and me. The newly arrived officers were welcomed and then the administrative officer, who was hosting the event on behalf of the absent CO, recognized the accomplishments of the LTJG. She received the Navy Achievement Medal for her accomplishments. Then it was my turn. I received the obligatory command plaque which I had paid for, and a blank Officer Fitness Report. No recognition was forthcoming for my achievements at Naval Submarine Base, San Diego.

As I left the room, it occurred to me that I should throw the plaque in the trash. I didn't, out of respect for the officers who remained at SUBASE.

Actually, my achievements at SUBASE were recognized in a back-handed way by the Navy's Inspector General some months later. Meanwhile, it was time to report to the USS Independence (CV62).

CHAPTER NINE

Chapter 9.1 USS Independence (CV-62)

I signed out of SUBASE, kissed the wife and kids goodbye, and got on a plane for Norfolk. The one really nice thing about the Navy is that every two or three years, you get a new beginning, although the past does have a way of following. To limit some of the fallout that might result from the SUBASE XO's trial, Captain Clint Smith, my former XO from Puerto Rico, who was assigned to the staff of the Commander, Naval Air Force, Atlantic (AIRLANT) called the CO of the *USS Independence* and vouched for my capability as a security officer and as a team player. It helped.

The *USS Independence* was the last of the Forrestal class super-carriers. It was also the fifth ship to be named *Independence.* She had a proud heritage. With a crew of 3950 people, she, like other carriers, was a floating city. She had been in overhaul at the Philadelphia Naval Shipyard from 1985 through mid-1988, so we conducted shakedown test cruises until August 15th when we set sail for the ship's new home port, San Diego. It's easy to fall into a routine on ships. I had an experienced chief petty officer, so I had very little law enforcement to do. Most of my work would be to attend meetings and do paperwork. During off duty hours in Norfolk, I did get to see Clint and Sue Smith and to go with them to Williamsburg, Virginia for the Independence Day celebrations.

The Master-at-Arms Division was part of the Administrative Department. My department head was a LDO lieutenant. That's a little like having a city chief of police answer to the personnel manager, or a sheriff answering to the county clerk. But that's the way it has almost always been, and you need to work within the system. My department head was easy to work for and with, so there were no real hardships. The XO, too, was easy to work with.

Aircraft carriers are so big that they give the impression of invulnerability. Nothing could be further from the truth. Their size is impressive, but they are also vulnerable to internal acts of terrorism and smuggling. A carrier is almost impossible to search thoroughly. There are voids that haven't been opened in years. A master-at-arms force of twenty or so men can't even begin to provide adequate physical security. Initially, I decided to concentrate on outside threats.

I got permission to formulate a sixty man auxiliary MA force. Although we had Marines on board, their duties were centered on the weapons systems. We needed an auxiliary force to repel boarders, and to back up the Master-at-Arms force. Most of the auxiliary force was made up of volunteers. They trained during off duty hours while we were at sea.

Radio communication between the Marines and the master-at- arms was non-existent. There was no central operations area to coordinate security-related response forces including, Marines, Master-at-Arms, and Weapons Department personnel. Nor had the three organizations practiced responding in a unified command. We did have encrypted radios, but the various organizations could not communicate with each other. I designated an area as an Emergency Operations Center, obtained new frequencies, and started to put a unified command system in place. Everyone knew how to do their jobs, but they were not used to doing their jobs with other organizations. We corrected that, creating a system of unified command similar to that used by civilian fire agencies, and more recently by the Department of Homeland Security.

USS Independence (CV-62)
U.S. Navy Photo

Chapter 9.2 Crossing the Equator – Making More Shellbacks

Since we would be going around the Cape Horn, we would cross the equator, which meant that we would once again have to turn slimy pollywogs into trusty shellbacks. Most of the 3950 men and officers on board were pollywogs. The day of the crossing was going to be a really long day.

During the planning meetings, I had asked that chief petty officers not actually needed in the ceremony be sent to the hangar bays where pollywogs would remain until they were ready for their turn at becoming shell backs. No problem, said the command master chief. No problem for him maybe, but no chiefs ever showed up. They were all on deck participating in the festivities. Evidently, yes can mean no in our country too.

Riots are easily started and nearly impossible to stop. Each division had its pollywogs waiting in the hangar bay. Shellback petty officers who were not part of the festivities were tormenting their pollywogs and some of the pollywogs were getting angry. To limit the potential for a riot, I passed the word that pollywogs had to remain seated, and shellbacks could only haze one man at a time. With limited personnel to keep order, the system worked. But no one likes sitting all day on hard steel decks. Everyone was glad when the crossing was over. I never did get topside to see the festivities.

Cape Horn is considered one of the world's most dangerous sea passages. It might seem that something as large as a carrier wouldn't be influenced by the seas. Unfortunately, that isn't the case. We lost most of our life rafts, many of our antennas, and other equipment. It was a rough passage. Several times we had to slow to thirteen knots because the seas were severely battering the ship's sponson.

Throughout the trip, the ship stopped at various ports. One of our first stops was at St. Thomas in the U.S. Virgin Islands. We were there for two days. I took my roommate, the executive officer of the Marine Detachment, to dinner. We had a prime rib so large that it wouldn't fit on the twelve inch plate and so thick that I wasn't sure we could eat it all. The next day I went to St John. It was still beautiful, but it wasn't the same without Pat.

Chapter 9.3 Sunset Parades

The various port visits were not just to give the crew some much needed rest. Rather, the ports were chosen by the State Department and the Navy so that the captain and the senior officers could meet with the host nation's officials.

To do that in a ceremonial yet social atmosphere, the ship's CO tasked the Marine Detachment with putting on a sunset parade in each port. The Marine Detachment XO (my roommate) acted as the parade CO, and I was to be the adjutant officer.

Sunset parades are a work of art. They started at a specific time before sunset and ended with taps being blown just as the sun set. They had to be timed perfectly. The parade was even more grand on a carrier than on a land-based parade ground because the Marines, dressed in battle gear with weapons, suddenly appeared as if by magic on one of the aircraft elevators. They moved in formation across the flight deck to their assigned position across from hundreds of visitors sitting in chairs on the flight deck. It was very patriotic and stirring, especially when the band played the National Anthems of the host country and of the United States.

Initially, there was some grumbling by the ship's Navy officers that I was the adjutant, while my roommate, who was junior to me, played the part of the parade commanding officer. That was never a problem for me because the adjutant had the better part to play. All of my experience with a sword (Manual of Arms) in military school when I was just a youngster, and later in boot camp paid off.

My roommate would yell, "Report."

I would then salute him with a sword salute, do an about face to face the crowd, salute the crowd, and then relate the history of the *USS Independence*. The ship's history took about ten minutes. I then invited ship's captain and civilian dignitaries to step forward and accept the parade's salute. The parade CO and the Marines implemented a series of troop movements and a rifle Manual of Arms, ending up with a salute to the captain and the dignitaries.

While we were conducting the sunset parade in St. Thomas, I completely forgot the script that I had memorized and had to ad lib. I went completely blank. I later apologized to the captain. He was gracious and said that he hadn't noticed. Right!

We put on a sunset parade in about six ports on the way to our new homeport. I didn't forget script in the other ports.

We arrived in San Diego on October 8, 1989. After 30 days of repairing the damages from the trip around Cape Horn, we began cruises along the coast of California. New personnel arrived who had to be trained in firefighting procedures and shipboard routines. The weeks passed quickly.

In January 1990, Captain Buzz Needham called me to his cabin. Once again, I had been issued new orders prematurely. I would be leaving the ship early for a new duty assignment that I knew nothing about. However, the captain was adamant about one point. He would not release me until he was rotated to his next command. We walked off the ship together.

Although Captain Needham and I have since retired from naval service. We still communicate by email on occasion. Captain "Buzz" Needham was another great CO under whom I was privileged to serve.

CHAPTER TEN

Chapter 10.1 Commander, Naval Base San Diego (CNBSD)

Months earlier, the Navy's Inspector General had visited each naval facility in the San Diego area and was able to enter every installation without proper identification except one: SUBASE. He questioned security personnel at SUBASE, asking who had designed and implemented the entry and security procedures. When the Inspector General returned to Washington D.C., he consulted with the Chief of Naval Operations and the Commander in Chief, U.S. Pacific Fleet. New orders were cut directing me to report to the staff of the Commander, Naval Base San Diego.

My orders specified that I was to coordinate and improve security at all naval installations in the San Diego area. That was not going to be an easy job. The resentment by installation security officers was intense. The fact was that the Naval base commander had no command authority over installation commanding officers. Like me, he was just a "coordinator."

I checked into CNBSD on March 1, 1989, and discovered that I would be working for Captain Bill Mackey who had been the CO of VC-8 in Puerto Rico when I was the security officer there. The admiral had no idea what to do with me, but since my orders were clear as to what I was to do, he was willing to let me design a regional security program.

The only way to improve security in the San Diego region was to get the cooperation of the installation commanding officers and security officers. To do that, I formulated a regional Physical Security

Review Board (PSRB) requiring all thirteen security officers from the naval installations to attend and participate. I outlined goals and objectives for the enhancement of security and antiterrorism. Then I got out of their way and let them meet the goals and objectives as best they could within their budget and staffing constraints.

Chapter 10.2 Readiness Versus Preparedness – The Rogers Incident

I have long believed that in public safety agencies, including emergency management, it is not enough to be prepared: We must be <u>ready</u>. To achieve readiness, there must be a systematic inspection program for personnel, procedures, and equipment. Few organizations want to implement a readiness program because departmental chiefs have no desire to admit the failures that exist within their public safety programs; military and civilian.

Nine days after I checked into CNBSD, Sharon Rogers was driving her van along Genesee Avenue in University City, a community within San Diego, when a bomb went off underneath her vehicle. Mrs. Rogers was stopped at a traffic light when she heard a noise. She looked in her rear view mirror and noticed that the back of the van was on fire. She unbuckled her seatbelt and calmly stepped out of the van, which continued to burn. That incident was important to the Navy because Mrs. Rogers was the wife of Captain Will Rogers, the commanding officer of the USS Vincennes (CG-49), which erroneously shot down an Iranian A300 Air Bus killing 290 passengers in the Persian Gulf on July 3, 1988.

> Investigation later revealed that the Iranians had removed the Identification Friend/Foe (IFF) radar device from an Iranian war plane, and installed it in the A300 Air Bus. To the USS Vincennes, the A300 looked like an enemy warplane on radar.

The bombing of the Rogers van proved conclusively that CNBSD was neither prepared nor ready to coordinate a response to an act of terrorism, or to any kind of major emergency. First, other than by commercial telephone, we had no instantaneous method for simultaneously contacting naval facilities in the San Diego area. Secondly, we had no operations or security personnel with which to make telephone calls. Even if we could contact each installation simultaneously, we could only recommend that they increase readiness because CNBSD had no command authority over installation commanding officers.

Photographer Unknown
This photo was given to me by a private citizen. The FBI came and got a copy later in the day. We were all looking for credible information.

Besides the fact that we didn't have personnel or equipment, we also didn't have an Emergency Operations Center (EOC) in which to coordinate operations. Our first concern was Naval Station San Diego where the USS Vincennes was moored. The Naval Station San Diego Security Officer increased security on the base and at the pier where the Vincennes was moored. I contacted the other naval facilities and asked them to increase security as well. It took a couple of hours to contact all of the facilities, and we took a great deal of criticism from the installations that were last on the call list.

We didn't have a direct line of communications with the FBI, NIS or even with the city of San Diego. We were just as much in the dark about what was happening as was everyone else.

We didn't know whether the bombing was really a terrorist act. We just weren't prepared, much less ready.

When Navy and Marine Corps installations tightened security, the first impact was to the city of San Diego. Normally, gate guards allowed vehicles to enter the installation based on the military decal on the car, and the identification card of the driver. Traffic moved fairly well. When security was increased, sentries looked at the identification card of the driver and all passengers. During high threats, guards must also inspect inside and underneath every vehicle entering and leaving bases.

This procedure took considerably more time and snarled city traffic. Because the bases are spread out all over the county, traffic was snarled in several areas of the city simultaneously. It wasn't long before I was getting calls from the city and then from the news media. They all wanted to know what I was going to do about the traffic. I was more concerned about the safety and the security of the naval facilities than I was about traffic snarled in the city.

The Rogers incident remains unsolved. There were several hypotheses, including one that said three Iranian students who were attending school in San Diego made and planted the bomb, then left the area. One of the reasons that this scenario seemed plausible was that the pipe bomb that was attached under the van was amateurishly made, as was the placement next to the catalytic converter, which caused the fire. The student hypothesis was not proved. The case remains open as far as I know.

The Rogers incident proved conclusively that CNBSD was not ready to handle an incident of any size. Working with the frequency coordinator, I was finally able to get an assigned radio frequency. Getting money for radios and antennas was even more difficult, but eventually, we did it. Getting the naval facilities to monitor the frequency and to respond when called was something else. Eventually even that got done.

Working with Captain Mackey, we set up an area for an Emergency Operations Center (EOC) and wrote instructions for staffing the various positions using personnel from CNBSD initially, and then expanding the EOC staff with personnel from various city, military, and federal agencies. We had not yet trained personnel to work in an EOC environment when we were hit by Red Cell, the Naval Security Coordination Team (NSCT), in what was to be a graded counterterrorism exercise.

Chapter 10.3 Red Cell Counterterrorism Exercises – Real, But Not Real

I have the greatest admiration and respect for Navy SEALs, but Red Cell, as a security testing program, was poorly structured. The whole idea behind Red Cell was to test the readiness and capability of naval facilities to repel attacks by terrorists. However, Red Cell was sorely needed. Few of the Navy brass, including shipboard and installation commanders, paid any real attention to the possibility of a terrorist attack, even though naval facilities in the Washington D.C. area had been targeted years earlier by domestic terrorists. Red Cell pointed out the vulnerabilities of the facilities being tested. What it didn't do was to provide answers as to how ships and installations could protect themselves.

The greatest fallacy of the Red Cell program was that the Navy Security Coordination Teams (NSCT), who played the aggressors in the exercise attacks on naval facilities, had the Navy's best trained personnel (Navy SEALs) and a large funding stream. Installation security was staffed by non-professionals and they had very low budgets. There were other fallacies too.

Basically, there are only two philosophies used for the protection or defense of a naval facility, especially large land-based installations: Don't allow the attacker to enter the facility. Don't allow the attacker to leave the facility.

Most naval installations can be infiltrated by a determined and disciplined person or persons at almost any time of the day or night. It doesn't take a highly trained and qualified team of Navy SEALs to enter an installation by stealth or cunning.

So it was that Red Cell invaded San Diego naval facilities. They arrived in San Diego, and were followed to their hotel by NCIS. When the exercise started, NCIS agents closed in, and apprehended the would-be terrorists. Exercise over! No, not really. The SEALs loudly yelled, FOUL.

NCIS received information that a group of terrorists would attack bases in San Diego during a particular timeframe. Without prior knowledge, they identified a particular group, tapped their phones, determined that they were in fact the terrorists, conducted liaison with the FBI and the police, and apprehended them before they could attack the bases. Isn't that what we pay them for? No, we had to allow the Red Cell to attack the bases, we were told.

The attacks had the predetermined affect – they wreaked havoc on the bases and the personnel. The real problem wasn't that the bases were not prepared or ready, we already knew that. The real problem with the RED Cell program was that security personnel didn't learn anything except that the SEALs could wreak havoc. We already knew that, too.

I got with the SEALs from Red Cell and asked that after they had wreaked their havoc, would they come back to the facility and reenact the scenario in slow motion, telling the defenders how they could have prevented the intrusion and how they should have reacted to protect the base.

Their answer was, "We don't know how to prevent an intrusion or protect a base. We only know how to insert, cause damage, and kill."

In short, nothing was accomplished; no learning took place. And that is why I say the Red Cell program was poorly designed. I would have loved to have had the opportunity to fix that.

The one good thing that came out of the Red Cell exercise was the positive endorsement of the CNBSD Emergency Operations Center (EOC). The SEALs were surprised that we had the capability to coordinate response and recovery with military and civilian agency personnel. The NSCT recommended that every base in the area adopt the EOC concept.

Chapter 10.4 Flushing the Admiral's Aide

One morning, soon after I had arrived at CNBSD, I was talking with Admiral Adams, the Naval Base Commander, about security-related issues. When I finished my briefing, I showed him a five and a quarter inch floppy disk. Now Admiral Adams, a naval aviator, liked a good joke. He was the kind of guy who would have fit in well with the Fun for Lunch Bunch at Roosevelt Roads. I explained the attributes of the program named "Flush."

His response was, "You should install that on the aide's computer."

I responded by saying, "you will have to distract the aide for a couple of minutes while I install the program.

The admiral agreed and called the aide into his office where the admiral explained that he was to give a speech at a luncheon in thirty minutes, and needed to have his notes typed right away.

The aide was the type of man who would be chosen for a Navy poster. He was tall, good looking, well-built and buff. He was also completely dedicated to the admiral.

When I had finished installing "Flush" on the aide's computer, I knocked on the door to the admiral's office asking if he was ready to see me. The admiral said he would see me after lunch. He then dismissed the aide, saying that there was precious little time to be wasted. He needed the typed notes immediately. I returned to my office, which was across the passageway from the admiral's office.

The aide started typing. When he had finished typing about three lines, the letters in the words at the end of the sentences that he was typing began falling to the bottom of the page.

At the bottom of the page, there was a swirling motion, which looked a lot like water going down a drain. The computer also made a sound like flushing a toilet. As the letters dropped to the bottom of the page, they disappeared. The aide typed faster and faster and the letters disappeared just as fast as he typed. The aide yelled, "Cline!"

Now why he would call me? I couldn't possibly have gotten a reputation for pranks that soon after my arrival at CNBSD. But nonetheless, he shouted my name again.

I entered his office and innocently asked, "What's up?" "What have you done to my computer?" he asked.

"Why, nothing," I responded, looking as innocent as I could.

"Damn it John, I have to get this speech typed for the admiral.

Don't mess with me."

"I have no idea what you're talking about," I said.

The admiral called the aide to his office and feigned anger at the slow progress that was being made getting his notes typed. The aide wanted to tell the admiral that I had screwed with his computer, but he didn't.

He said only, "I'm having difficulty with my computer." "Let me see," said the admiral.

The admiral walked out to the aide's office and sat in the chair in front of the aide's computer. Letters were still falling from the typed paragraph.

"I see no problem," said the admiral.

The aide responded by saying, "sir, the letters are falling to the bottom of the page and disappearing."

"What's that flushing sound I hear coming out of your computer, lieutenant?"

"I don't know," said the exasperated aide looking at me desperately.

"Hmmm, said the admiral, who suddenly pushed the F1 key, thereby restoring the entire sheet of typed notes.

Then he said, "The problem is lieutenant, you've been flushed."

Several of the officers on the staff had gathered around the admiral as he had begun troubleshooting the aide's computer. They all laughed.

The aide looked at me and said, "I'll get you for this."

Yes, the admiral was a prankster too. And no, he didn't really have a speech to give. Rather, he bought lunch for his very aggravated aide in an effort to calm him down.

Over the next few years, several admirals came and went, as Commander, Naval Base, San Diego. None were as nice as Admiral Adams.

Admiral Adams, CNBSD (Photo by John Cline)

Chapter 10.5 PACEX-89

Following on the heels of the marauding SEALs of Red Cell came the Pacific Fleet Exercise of 1989. Where the SEALs had attacked selected naval facilities, PACEX-89 would attack civilian seaports and military installations throughout the Pacific area of operations. My job was to keep the exercise participants in San Diego safe. To do that, I had to plan the Orange Force operations. I finally got to be the bad guy again. I also had to plan, implement, and coordinate White Cell operations, those people who evaluate and judge the effectiveness of an attack and the subsequent responses. Planning was the easy part. Implementing and coordinating both the attackers and the evaluators was tough. I didn't get any real sleep for well over a week. What little sleep I did get was on a couch in my office.

In San Diego, attacks were conducted during nighttime only so that we would not adversely impact city traffic. We started slowly, with attacks on individual port operations and military installations. By the end of the week, we were attacking everything in sight simultaneously. At sea, elements of the Pacific Fleet, including Canadian ships, were defending the western coast from a fleet of Orange force vessels. It was a huge exercise. When the excise ended, we had to put together a list of lessons learned. We did learn a lot from the exercise.

Chapter 10.6 Desert Shield and Desert Storm

In 1991, I received another call from the detailer. He said something to the effect of, since I had already been to the Persian Gulf, would I be interested in returning to support Desert Shield and Desert Storm, the military action by thirty four allied nations under a United Nations mandate?

"Yes," I said.

"No," said the admiral.

One of the more serious concerns in San Diego during Desert Shield and Desert Storm was that Iraqis who had immigrated to the United States might be sympathetic to the cause of Saddem Hussein. There was a fear that sympathizers would use Improvised Explosive Devices (IEDs) to attack military and civilian infrastructure in support of Iraq. The Navy had only a few bomb detection dogs, and the civilian police had even fewer. Explosives Ordnance Disposal technicians were in great demand. The use of military resources became a coordination nightmare. Bombs, real and imagined, were sighted all over the county. By the time the war was over, six pipe bombs had been found in the San Diego area, far fewer than was expected.

Although coordinating requests for military resources was time consuming, useable information became my biggest problem. People wanted to know when and if they were in danger. Police needed to know what was going on so that they could react to incidents before those incidents became disasters.

The FBI was not prone to providing intelligence, and the NCIS was equally protective of information that they had acquired. Everyone was playing "I have a secret." Breaking down the barriers and developing non-classified useable information that could be shared with public safety agencies was a major headache. We were determined to provide legitimate threat assessments so that both military and civilian public safety officials and military commanders could implement a satisfactory level of safety and security for their constituents. We developed and dispensed three public safety threat assessments every day – one in the morning, one in the afternoon, and one at midnight. It was a very successful and well received program.

The news media, CNN especially, was no help. They were looking for sensationalism. Unwittingly, I became the antiterrorism voice for the Commander, Naval Base San Diego. While being interviewed about the use of IEDs in San Diego, the CNN reporter said that he would not ask me what specific security measures were being implemented at naval installations. We agreed that any other question except the implementation of security measures was open for discussion.

Standing on a Navy pier in downtown San Diego with the backdrop of the harbor and Naval Air Station North Island in the background, CNN was doing a live feed. Sure enough, the last question asked was, "What specific security measures are you taking to ensure the safety of the military and civilian public?"

I answered that I would not provide that information for obvious reasons.

When the live feed broke away, I asked the reporter why he asked the one question we had agreed would not be asked.

He answered, "I thought the public needed to hear you say that you wouldn't talk about specific security measures."

I learned then that you just can't trust a member of the news media – no matter what they tell you in advance. There is no such thing as "off the record" either. I now view reporters as a pack of jackals, which is too bad because I was one once.

Chapter 10.7 The Mount Pinatubo Eruption – Operation Fiery Vigil

In June of 1991, Mount Pinatubo, a volcano just fifty five miles northwest of the capitol city of Manila, in the Philippine Islands erupted, killing hundreds of people, and displacing hundreds of thousands of people. Clark Air Force Base was particularly hard hit by volcanic debris, and its personnel had to be evacuated. Most of the personnel from Naval Station Subic Bay and Cubi Point were also evacuated. All over the United States, military coordinators were establishing a network of USO and military personnel to help the thousands of military personnel and their dependents, some of whom who had lost important documents and needed the basic necessities of life.

Because San Diego is a coastal city and a Navy town, it was heavily travelled by evacuated sailors and their families. Operation Fiery Vigil was the largest peacetime evacuation of military personnel ever carried out.

Once again, we activated the EOC. We established a twenty- four hour military presence at Lindbergh Field where Navy representatives met every arriving flight to ensure that evacuees, those who needed assistance, got what they needed. For many, that was simply getting them to another flight. For others, it meant getting with a military paymaster so that the evacuees could get money to live on or to continue travelling. Sometimes it meant recreating official documents including service records, so we would have to get the evacuee to a personnel office. Some evacuees had lost nearly everything and had to start over from scratch. It took a couple of weeks for all of the evacuees to be processed.

One day several months later, we received word that the Navy was going to send personnel and families back to Subic Bay and Cubi Point. We had twelve hours to implement the coordination for the return of sailors and their families travelling through San Diego to the Philippines.

Chapter 10.8 Ridden Hard and Put Away Wet

Emergency Management was largely ignored by the Navy, even more so than was security. Yet, because prevention, response, and recovery programs are important tools that are employed before, during, and after a natural or man-caused disaster, it was necessary to test the capability of each naval facility in the CNBSD area of responsibility to ensure that they could implement those programs in case of earthquake or other disaster. To accomplish those tests, we formed an Emergency Management Inspection Team using active duty personnel and Navy Liaison Officers. NLOs were Naval Reserve captains and commanders who were assigned to emergency management billets.

Because the active duty Navy ashore takes off on weekends during peacetime, there was little for the NLOs to do on drill weekends. Captain Mackey asked me to design and implement an emergency management training program tailored specifically for our NLOs. There were a number of courses and schools available, and when no class was available, I taught weekend classes. NLOs assigned to CNBSD were eager to be productive members of the Navy, so it was an easy fix. In a short time, they became expert in all three programs: Preparedness, Response, and Recovery, studying even when they weren't on Navy time. They even came up with life-saving information that wasn't in the books.

The look on the faces of installation commanders when they met the Emergency Management Inspection Team always struck me as being comical. The team consisted of five or six Navy captains, two or three commanders, and one lieutenant commander – me. I was always the junior officer. Sometimes our civilian employee, who was an Emergency Management Technician, would join the inspection team. The look on the faces of installation commanders almost always displayed instant panic.

One such inspection was to be held at the Naval Training Command (NTC). We entered the captain's office where we were to provide him with the pre-inspection brief. He took one look at the number of captains and commanders, and literally ran out of the office. We had never had that reaction before.

We waited for about ten minutes. Finally, the captain's superior, a rear admiral, walked in and told us that there would be no inspection that day. They knew that their Emergency Management program was not ready for an inspection. Because the Navy didn't place very much emphasis on emergency management, they never envisioned that a professional team, a team that really knew what they were doing, would conduct the inspection. The installation commander feared that failing the inspection would be career ending. But we didn't work that way, although our inspection reports were very comprehensive. We agreed to work with base personnel and to conduct an inspection during the following year. For official purposes, we decided to label our presence as an "assist visit" not an inspection.

Part of the inspection was a drill. Personnel would not know in advance what type of disaster we would throw at them. They had to respond to the disaster and demonstrate that they had the capability to save lives and recover from the disaster, while simultaneously retaining the capability to go to war, if required.

Few installations could handle the added communication requirements. Even fewer had a plan to protect the children at schools and learning centers on the bases. It was a learning experience for everyone.

When I retired from the Navy, the NLOs gave me a stirrup mounted on a plaque. The insinuation was that I had ridden them hard and put them away wet. That was not true. They were always way ahead of me. They were another exceptional group of naval officers who, by and large, were not adequately recognized for their exceptional contributions to the United States Navy.

Chapter 10.9 Retiring from the Navy

I read somewhere that we retire when we reach the moment of complete dissatisfaction. I watched as people wrestled with the notion of retiring from the Navy, and in almost every case, retirement followed some incident that caused them to feel that they could no longer continue to serve an uncaring master. Certainly that was true for me.

When I went to the Persian Gulf, I was promised that when I reached the end of my next tour, I would get the commanding officer billet at the Master-at-Arms School at Lackland Air Force Base in San Antonio, Texas. A few days before I was to execute new orders, I called the detailer saying that I still had not received written orders to Lackland AFB. There was a long pause, and then the detailer told me that I was going to Italy, not Texas.

Two situations were at play to cause the change in orders. One, there was an urgent need to replace a security officer in Italy because he had gotten into trouble with the local mafia. Secondly, the CO billet at Lackland AFB was a female administrative officer billet. The detailer and NCIS wanted a security officer to fill the position, but the Training Command admiral who controlled that billet would not allow it to be changed. I was invited to call the admiral to see if I could get him to change his mind.

I knew that particular admiral because he had been the Commander, Naval Air Force, U.S. Pacific Fleet at NAS North Island, and I spent the first part of every morning briefing him about threat assessments during Desert Shield and Desert Storm. I called him and got nowhere. I reminded him that the last three administrative officers had been fired. Still he would not relent. I called the detailer and told him that I was unable to get the admiral to change his mind. The detailer told me to pack my bags for Italy.

Every naval officer wants his own command. The Master-at-Arms School at Lackland AFB was at that time the only possibility for a physical security officer to achieve command except maybe at a Navy brig. Now that the Training Command admiral would not allow me to fill the Master-at-Arms School CO billet, achieving command was no longer a possibility for me.

My wife and I had made the decision earlier that when it came time to retire from the Navy, we would settle in Austin, Texas. After the Navy, I would seek employment with the state's disaster services organization. All of our future plans had been made around the Lackland AFB assignment, which was not to be. So, I had reached that moment of complete dissatisfaction.

I would have enjoyed a tour in Italy if I had been a few years younger. My wife's mother was sickly and would die within the next year. Pat felt that she should stay with her. The detailer said that I could go to Italy on an "unaccompanied tour" without dependents. If I went to Europe, I wanted the family to gain the experience too. But we could not afford for my wife to travel back and forth between Europe and San Diego as her mother's health deteriorated. I told the detailer that I would get back with him the next day. Meanwhile, I spent the rest of the day looking into retirement options. I found an option that the Navy could not change or prevent. It would allow me to retire ten months after I submitted retirement papers.

Pat and I talked about the assignment in Italy until midnight. We just couldn't find a satisfactory solution to meet the needs of the family. Then I casually mentioned that I could retire, thus allowing us to stay in San Diego. We talked until two in the morning. When I got to the office the next morning, I submitted my retirement papers and called the detailer saying that I would not execute the orders to Italy as I was retiring from the Navy. He hung up on me.

Reaction to my retirement was astonishing to me. The admiral I worked for told me that I was making a bad mistake. One admiral called me to say that I was being disrespectful of the naval service that had given me so much, while another admiral called and said that I was being traitorous.

I received orders allowing me to remain at CNBSD for the remaining ten months until I retired. But the work environment changed. My security clearance was pulled, so I could no longer participate in any meeting requiring a clearance, and almost all meetings did require a clearance. So for nearly ten months, I did very routine jobs of little or no importance. Once again, I was persona non grata.

Partially because of the reaction I received when I submitted my retirement papers, I decided to have a formal retirement ceremony. I requested the Navy band. Because I was ten months early, I easily got on the band's schedule, as long as no admiral or captain preempted me. I made arrangements to have the ceremony on the lawn at the Admiral Kidd Club on the Naval Training Center so that we could have the reception inside the club. I asked several of the security officers in San Diego to be my side boys (ceremonial honor guard); only one or two showed up. We sent invitations to everyone we knew. Based on the RSVP list, we expected about one hundred guests.

I arrived an hour before the scheduled ceremony. Nothing was set up; not the chairs, not the podium, nothing. I started setting out chairs because the guests were arriving.

The working party finally arrived and I was relieved of setting up chairs. The band arrived, set up, and started playing. By the appointed hour, everything was in readiness. It was time to formally and ceremoniously leave the United States Navy.

About 200 people showed up for the ceremony. Captain Mackey who had retired a year earlier was my principle speaker. He chose not to wear his uniform, but wore a suit instead. The FBI sent a representative who presented me with a plaque from the Bureau. The Section Manager for the American Radio Relay League, the organization that represents the nation's ham radio operators, also presented me with a plaque.

My coworker and friend, Sam Whitteker, a retired Navy Master Chief, who was then a civilian employee, and who took my place as Regional Security Officer, made an enormous "shadow box" with my ribbons, brass plates listing all of my assignments, and a large ceremonial flag that had flown over CNBSD. The Command Master Chief presented the shadow box, indicating that it was the largest one that he had ever seen. It was certainly the largest shadow box I have ever seen too. Then it was time to "swallow the anchor". Patsy and I walked across the ceremonial brow, paused for the bos'n pipe and final salute, and paused in respect as the band played "God Bless America".

We went to the reception at the Admiral Kidd Club where I chatted with the guests. Captain Keathley and his wife Billie honored us by coming to the ceremony from Florida on their annual trek to San Francisco. A chief petty officer I never expected to see showed up. We had worked together at SUBASE when he was a first class petty officer. I was glad to see him again. I saw a lot of other friends and acquaintances too – and then suddenly, it was all over. I was a civilian again.

We found a civilian rental and moved out of Navy housing. Over the remaining years, we have learned the difference between military and civilian friends.

CIVILIAN FRIENDS: Are for a while (out of sight means, out of mind).

MILITARY FRIENDS: Are for life (the stories just get better with every telling).

www.ingramcontent.com/pod-product-compliance
Lightning Source LLC
Chambersburg PA
CBHW021355090426
42742CB00009B/870